# SAFER CITIES OF THE FUTURE

*Rise Up, Clip On, and Grow Out*

*for a Better Urban Experience*

ALLAN BONNER

Safer Cities of the Future

First printing, July, 2015

Published by Sextant Publishing, Edmonton, Alberta, Canada

© Allan Bonner, BA, BEAD, MA, MSc, DBA, LLM, MScPl (Cand.)

Printed in Canada by Friesens Printing

Book Design and Layout by Dean Pickup, CanadaBookDesign.com

Cover Image: Our Cities Ourselves / Institute for Transportation and Development Policy / ©

ISBN: 978–1–926755–13–7 (soft cover)
ISBN: 978-1-926755-14-4 (hard cover)

For educational or institutional discounts or for information about
seminars and speeches, please contact:

Sextant Publishing, Edmonton, Alberta, Canada
or
www.allanbonner.com
1–416–961–3620

# Praise for Allan Bonner's *Safer Cities of the Future*

"In this work, Bonner highlights how urban planners, public administrators and emergency managers often work within their own silos, often to the detriment of public health, safety and urban sustainability.  Safer Cities of the Future breaks down these barriers and presents a manual to guide urban professionals on key aspects of creating safe and sustainable cities."

**John L. Renne, Ph.D., AICP**
Associate Provost of Urban Initiatives and Director of Merritt C. Becker Transportation Institute,
University of New Orleans; Senior Visiting Research Associate, University of Oxford

"Allan Bonner's *Safer Cities of the Future* takes its readers on an illuminating and engaging tour through the emergency plans of 100 cities in North America, the United Kingdom, and Australia. Its findings will surprise you. In an era where over half of the world's population lives in cities, and catastrophic weather events are becoming the 'new normal,' the need for an honest account of our emergency planning efforts is apparent. Safer Cities is a challenge to the planning profession and its accredited schools to integrate urban crisis management into city building processes and core curricula. The book not only lays out the extent of the problem, it offers numerous solutions. It does so brilliantly."

**Julia Markovich,**
Visiting Scholar, Geography & Program in Planning, University of Toronto

"...valuable points about emergency planning, including evacuation..."

**Senator Art Eggleton,**
Toronto's longest serving Mayor

# Table of Contents

# Acknowledgements

As I've written in this spot in other books, I've often found the thanks to helpers does not ring true – false modesty, pro forma lists of people and taking responsibility where it is obviously required.

On this occasion though, there is some serious responsibility to be taken and gratitude due. This will also serve as product labeling for the reader – a disclaimer that may not please some cities we put under the microscope, but will inform readers of what we saw.

First, my responsibility. I am lucky to travel through many of the great cities of the world regularly. This, and having lived in many Canadian cities, caused my long–standing interest in urban affairs. What takes me to cities is my consulting practice in communication and crisis management. So, I'm on the lookout for urban issues to research and discuss.

While writing a paper for the planning department at the University of Toronto, I skimmed my city's emergency plan. I was shocked to find no substantial information about evacuation, other than it's a tough decision to make. This was years after people lost their lives in New Orleans trying to leave the city, staying put or being prevented from leaving.

My training in crisis management tells me that you try to make all decisions you can in advance. Standing in an intersection clogged with traffic during a weather or terror event is no time to be trying to decide whether to tell residents to stay put or get out of town. The least you try to do is define the circumstances under which you do call for shelter in place or evacuation.

I was motivated to find out more.

I must confess that my choice of methodology was influenced by the work of Richard Florida. I'm 'confessing' because as a scientist and researcher I'm not entirely pleased with the use of focus groups and proxies (guesses, often) to parse complex human behaviour. But there's no doubt that Florida's lists and rankings of cities has garnered attention, and that's what the topic of urban safety needs.

Then came the question of how to compile my lists of cities – ranked by safety and preparedness criteria. There's no point in asking people who know little or nothing about a topic to express detailed views – there's too much of that in research these days. There's no point in asking those in charge to rank their own work. Police, fire, EMS and the mayor's office will probably determine they're doing all they can with budgets available. I experimented with a number of methods before settling on a simulation of sorts.

The simulation was inspired by something I've experienced dozens of times. I regularly get calls from junior to mid–level managers who have been asked by their bosses to write or update their crisis plans. They don't know where to start, what's available or what best practices are. I point them to my text and interactive DVD on the topic and also offer my critique and other help.

I decided to simulate the head of a non–governmental association, business, school, college, hospital, high–rise or other organization wanting to be prepared. One of the first steps would be to see what's in my city's emergency plan and see if it provided guidance. So, I asked a group of students who were working for me to print out emergency plans from the 100 largest cities in the English–speaking world. I omitted some suburbs and added some cities in Australia, the UK and Canada which were a little small to be on the list, but which were of special interest to me.

The students were well qualified for this task. They had backgrounds in media studies, urban planning and law. This was a realistic assignment for them. The search and the downloading began.

There are obvious flaws in this simulation, as there would be in a real assignment to find the city's emergency plan. The search and downloading took about a month. It's conceivable that a plan may have been updated the day after my researcher found and printed it. Our review that it's old or deficient may only capture a moment in time. But with 100 plans to review, we think our general observations about age of plans and deficiencies will be pretty accurate.

We double and triple checked when we found little of significance on a city's website. Some researchers found material that others had missed. Some who prefer reading on the web versus on paper found new material. Nonetheless, when we recorded that a plan was lacking or deficient, it was after several tries to find substantial information by several people. We think that's worth noting because we think that few would show the tenacity that my team did.

I also take responsibility for making a judgment call on how accessible a plan is. For some, a drop-down or pop-up menu is evidence of completeness and flexibility driven by users. For others, these tools obscure text on the printed page. Similarly, maps are useful, but without street names I wonder why they've been included.

I made judgment calls about other matters on the advice of my team. I don't expect much of an argument about jargon, acronyms, hyper–clarity, lists of civic leaders and other matters that don't keep anyone safer. We had good, but unresolved discussions about whether users would search for their city's plans by name (Toronto's Emergency Plan) or by topic (Toronto's advice on making a 'go–bag'). In the end, you have to know your city has an emergency plan or what a 'go–bag' is before you search for either. Does a city using its own bandwidth for videos show more social media savvy than one that uses YouTube? Is signing up for social media messages evidence of wise use of these tools, or about to be outdated because of reverse social media messages (much like reverse 911 calls)? We tried to give points for cognizance of the importance of social media, but hesitated after considering that sending messages about a power outage over devices that need power is at least ironic. We made lists accordingly.

That's all my responsibility. Now the credit. Kerron Williams found the plans and then found more details on ones that looked a little light. Kerron also searched for video and the use of other social media. I read about 20 plans and Saad Malik read the other 80 and prepared a one–page briefing note, as he might have for his boss in industry or government. I then went back and read the notes and the rest of the plans. Saad also cross–referenced what we had in print with what he found online in later months.

Ashley McIntosh emailed and called the 100 emergency managers. Darnel Harris spot–checked our reading of plans, proofread the manuscript, sourced the photos and images in this book and secured the rights to them. He also updated our search after a year of working on the data. Both Saad and Darnel worked on creating accessible guidance for citizens who might want to be better prepared with first aid, evacuation protocols, and the ability to stay put. Teoman Pontais worked on our on–line courses in English and French and edited our video content. Amanda Lau designed and constructed the Safer Cities tab with open sourced material.

Now, on to the older students. After a 40 year career in journalism in top posts in London, Washington and Moscow, Hal Jones joined me as both a fellow student and a teacher of communication and crisis management. He's also been my editor, turning both rambling thoughts and impenetrable academic work into accessible material for our clients. Dale Johnson is both a student and teacher, and he's a great teacher in both my company and in university classes. Dale fine–tuned our on–line courses. Oxonian and Harvardian, Dr. Roy Damary, my doctoral supervisor, also fine–tuned our on–line courses for possible use in Russia.

I'm grateful for the encouragement of my University of Toronto Urban Planning instructors who endured early drafts and short versions of this book. Kanishka Goonewardena inspired a tone of post–modernism.

Sue Ruddick's assignment inspired the look at the fictional Toronto neighbourhood in 2092. Julia Markovich's transport class and David Hulchanski's simultaneous individual instruction gave me the impetus to incorporate supporting academic literature and get a final manuscript into some kind of acceptable shape for editing. Ryan Hum endured a class presentation in which I used the monorail scene from the Simpsons to justify redundant transport. Others just endured, notably Paul Hess.

All the while I received unexpected and unearned support from two significant sources – not instructors in a university or with any job description to justify their support. One is long–standing colleague Bob Millward, who has been referred to in the newspaper as a "legendary planner." We met while he was Toronto's Commissioner of Planning and kept up a friendship through regular lunches. I have vetted my ideas with him regularly and have had an enormous boost from his encouragement.

Senator Art Eggleton, the longest–serving mayor in Toronto's history, falls into this category too. We met briefly 30 years ago when I was executive assistant to the world's longest–serving big city Mayor – Mel Lastman of North York. Later, when Mayor Eggleton became minister of national defence, I had been working for his department for many years and got bumped up to some projects in his office. We've kept up a friendship over lunches and email exchanges. He's been very encouraging to me, but always cautions against some of my ideas which might disrupt neighbourhoods – and that's part of how you get re–elected regularly.

I've written elsewhere about my gratitude to Simon Bennett and Leicester University – home of the first and best Risk, Crisis and Disaster Management program in the world. We've kept up a friendship and I'm grateful for his regular email exchanges about crises around the world, and for his introduction to this book.

Speaking of enduring, every now and then I get up from my reading or writing and ask my wife, Lorna, for her ruling on usage, an approach or other matters. I discuss these kinds of matters with my sons, Christian and Michael – both with their own expertise in popular culture and public policy. Their input is much appreciated.

In final sentences to these acknowledgements, I'm supposed to add the pro–forma statement that 'errors and omissions are mine.' But when lives are at stake, I must modify this. The faults in research design are mine, but the errors and omissions we found in municipal emergency plans are the responsibility of the writers of those plans whose responsibility it is to save lives. As British academic Brian Toft has written, we "owe" it to those who have lost their lives to do all we can to prevent further loss. This research indicates that there is much more to do.

# Foreword

Dr Simon Bennett,
Director Civil Safety and Security Unit, University of Leicester, Leicester, UK

Our world is shaped by forces we cannot control. Two such forces are urbanisation and globalisation. By 2050, around three quarters of the world's population will live in cities. That is, by 2050, seven billion people will live out their lives on a mere 2% of the global land mass. Such a concentration of population will have major implications for the way we think about and manage cities. Globalisation has seen the creation of a single, communications–supported global economy where capital chases the highest net profit regardless of social cost. In his seminal 1998 book *Globalisation – The Human Consequences*, sociologist Zygmunt Bauman talks of 'unanchored power': "It is up to [shareholders] to move the company wherever they spy out or anticipate a chance of higher dividends, leaving to all others – locally bound as they are – the task of wound–licking, damage–repair and waste–disposal. The company is free to move; but the consequences of the move are bound to stay. Whoever is free to run away from the locality, is free to run away from the consequences. These are the most important spoils of victorious space war."

In 2015, capitalism – a mode of production where the means of production are controlled by an empowered minority – reigns supreme. Almost beyond political control, the new oligarchs and corporate boards are free to squeeze every last drop of effort from employees. British commentator William Hutton described this exploitative arrangement as long ago as 1995. In *The State*

*We're In: Why Britain Is in Crisis and How to Overcome It*, Hutton wrote: "Firms, anxious to meet their shareholders' requirements for high returns, have taken advantage of the deregulation of the labour market to impose more casualised, part–time, 'flexible' patterns of work and so increase their capacity to modify their costs to the changing pattern of demand. Only around 40 per cent of the work–force enjoy tenured, full–time employment or secure self–employment … another 30 per cent are insecurely self–employed, involuntarily part time or casual workers; while the bottom 30 per cent, the marginalised, are idle or working for poverty wages." Britain's current Prime Minister is fond of trumpeting how many 'new jobs' his coalition government has created. He is noticeably reluctant to discuss what types of jobs have been created – for the most part low–paid, insecure service–sector jobs.

Unchecked, urbanization and globalisation will produce mega–cities inhabited for the most part by poorly–paid workers on short–term or pay–by–the–hour contracts. These workers will live in overcrowded, poorly–serviced and jerry–built accommodation – because they cannot afford anything better. Their children will attend schools where they will be taught just enough to get by – because what is the point of educating the sons and daughters of the underclass? Chances are they won't do anything with their lives, save follow in their parents' footsteps, if they are lucky. Perhaps the most extreme manifestation of this form of urbanization is the favela (shanty–town). Rio's favelas were either hidden behind hoardings or bulldozed for the 2014 World Cup. They endure – breeding grounds for criminality, ignorance and inequality. And this in a country where a series of left–leaning governments have promised to do something about them.

It would be wrong to assume that the developing world has a monopoly on urban dysfunction. Civic decay – and in the case of Detroit, Michigan, near civic collapse – is a feature of the social, economic and political landscape of the world's most powerful economy. Because it usually occurs over a long period of time (in Detroit's case over a period of some 40 years) civic decay is difficult to spot, analyse, and rectify. In Detroit's case, the riots of 1967 were a wake–up call. They showed that Motor City had a dark and rather unpleasant underbelly. They showed that even when minorities made a significant contribution to the city economy, old prejudices persisted. Pre–riot tensions and inequalities were systematically glossed over by the authorities, as illustrated by the commentary to the 1965 J.T. Slayden–directed documentary *Detroit: City On The Move*:

"Detroit is enjoying its finest hour. There is a renaissance, a rebirth in the city. There is a newness in Detroit."

"There is a resurgence of civic pride and unfettered imagination. A new renaissance is changing the face of the city. This renaissance, seen everywhere, is the direct result of considered planning."

"Detroit, an exciting place to ... work shoulder–to–shoulder regardless of national origin, colour or creed. Detroit has earned an outstanding record in community relations."

"The friendliness of its people reaches out ... the dedication to progress – social, spiritual, cultural and material is equalled only by its Twentieth Century Vision."

The documentary's denialist gloss hid an ugly reality: Detroit was a city with a simmering race–relations problem that went unchallenged by a mostly white and, some would argue, institutionally racist police force. The 1967 riots, which lasted five days and nights, saw 33 blacks and 10 whites killed and over 7,200 people arrested. Approximately 2,500 stores were looted and the total property damage was estimated at $32 million. A shock to the city's psyche, the riots planted the first seeds of doubt that Detroit had a future as a popular and successful manufacturing city. Today we know what happened. Over the decades, jobs and people moved out, drugs and crime moved in, the tax base shrunk and, in July 2013, the city went bankrupt owing 100,000 creditors $18 billion (£12 billion).

Detroit's fall from grace has left the city on its knees, socially, economically and politically. In 2011 the proportion of New York's denizens living in poverty stood at 19.4%. The number of Detroit's denizens living in poverty stood at 36.2%. In New York there were 6 murders per 100,000 people. In Detroit there were 48. In 2000, unemployment in Detroit stood at 7.3%, a level that was just about sustainable. By 2012 it had risen to 18.6%. The city's problems were compounded by what can only be described as an exodus. At its 1950 apogee, Detroit was a city of nearly two million people. Many of these had skilled or semi–skilled jobs in the auto industry. By 2012, the city held just 685,000 souls, many of whom lacked the education and skills demanded by America's increasingly high–technology New Millennium economy. A city like Detroit presents civil servants with enormous challenges, like securing the funds to maintain and exercise one's emergency plans. A bankrupt Town Hall will be more interested in securing inward investment than in developing emergency plans for a shrinking population.

Other cities may not face challenges as severe as those faced by Detroit, but, as Zygmunt Bauman warns, no hamlet is immune from the chill wind of economic restructuring. Unanchored capital is drawn to locations with the most skilled, best qualified and least troublesome workforces. Countries with pools of unorganised, quiescent, low–paid yet well–educated labour are a more attractive proposition than countries with organised, expectant labour. The BRIC phenomenon is a direct result of capital mobility. Countries like Brazil, Russia, India and China attract old money like a magnet attracts steel pins. And there is very little the old world can do about it, save rein in workers' rights, lower expectations and hope for the best. Britain may have weathered the post–2007 economic storm better than many countries, but only at the expense of a collapse in living standards due partly to casualisation.

Of course, it would be wrong to attribute all our cities' woes to economic forces like globalisation, capital mobility and the economic cycle. Cities attract not only the most talented and entrepreneurial, but also the most desperate and devious. As Charles Dickens observed of Victorian London, criminality thrives in dense, anonymous conurbations. In 1824 at the age of eleven, Dickens found himself living alone in lodgings and in danger of joining London's thriving criminal underclass. He would wander the streets, simultaneously repulsed and attracted by the anarchy. "What wild visions of prodigies of wickedness, want and beggary arose in my mind out of that place" he wrote. Nothing changes. Cities remain wicked places. Their febrility *invites* wickedness. Dickens's London had the Artful Dodger and Fagin's miscreants (accurate fictional representations of Victorian London's criminal underclass). Today's Great Wen has larcenous bankers, violent drug gangs, car–jackers, football hooligans, phone–hacking journalists, credit–card scammers, greedy police officers, terrorists who seek publicity through intimidation and mass–murder and, reportedly, professional beggars who earn £50,000 per annum.

London's woes are as nothing compared to those of an exploding metroplex like Rio de Janeiro. While Rio is benefitting from Brazil's rise to world power status – Brazil is forecast to become the world's fifth largest economy by 2026 – it remains a city of social division and blighted lives. Rio hosts Rocinha, Brazil's largest favela. Rocinha houses up to 180,000 of Rio's poorest. From a distance Rocinha looks picturesque as it clings to the mountainside. Close–up it presents a less attractive face, with poor–quality housing, open sewers and narrow alleys. Lacking any form of rational planning, Rocinha is a nightmare for the police and Rio's emergency services. Across Brazil over eleven million people (equivalent to the population of Portugal) live in favelas – a civic risk–management challenge *par excellence*.

Brazil's favela problem pales into insignificance compared to that of India, where the 2011 census identified around 64 million slum–dwellers. The fact that roughly one–third of India's 1.2 billion people live in urban slums creates a huge public safety problem. Slums speed the spread of disease and fire. They offer cover for criminals, addicts and other miscreants. They hamper efforts to get every child a basic education. They create access problems for the emergency services. More than one–third of India's slum homes have no indoor toilet and two–thirds are not connected to the sewerage system. Paradoxically, the census noted that 70 percent of slum households had televisions and 64 percent had cellphones.

Under–pressure cities and the people who inhabit them are not easily managed. In terms of ensuring public safety and security they present enormous challenges. All the more surprising, then, that many are failing to develop relevant and effective emergency plans. As the author of *Safer Cities of the Future* writes: "I selected 100 cities in the developed and English speaking world and asked to study their emergency preparedness plans …. I am not convinced that those given the task of preparing these plans have come to grips with the extent and magnitude of the problems they may confront. All too often clear instructions in plain language were avoided in favour of bureaucratic jargon sprinkled liberally with baffling acronyms." Some cities were failing to regularly review and update their emergency plans. An out–of–date plan is a recipe for anarchy.

I commend this book because it not only highlights complacency, but also offers solutions. In *Seven Stages of Planning* the author offers us a policy–making model that references several types of knowledge, including that which resides in the populace. As Professor Brian Wynne discovered in his analysis of the UK Government's lamentable response to radioactive fallout from the 1986 Chernobyl reactor fire, local knowledges – in this case Cumbrian hill farmers' insights into weather and grazing patterns and the nature of hilltop vegetation – are often overlooked by technocrats. The author writes: "Citizen engagement is a fundamental value in planning." The author's critique of the planning process should be read by every civic emergency planning team, and every student of emergency planning.

Further on in the book the author addresses the problem of mitigating risk in the burgeoning mega–slums of the Twenty–First Century. He offers several solutions, from making potable water with the aid of a simple chlorine dispenser, to charging small devices with a dynamo powered by the steam from a kettle. Regarding the problems faced by mega–slums he notes: "Planning for the future isn't always easy but it has to be easier in our 'developed' world than anywhere else. Compared to the difficulties facing the rest of the world we have little to complain about and our challenges are marginal." A truer word was never spoken.

I shall make one final observation. While both the developed and developing world have problems, we must remember that, overall, the human condition is improving. The London that a foot–slogging eleven year–old Charles Dickens got to know no longer exists. Globally, people are better off today than they were one hundred years ago. The 2014 Organisation for Economic Co–operation and

Development (OECD) report *How Was Life? Global Well–being Since 1820* notes that literacy levels now approach 100% "almost everywhere." The report also notes that at the start of the Industrial Revolution, life expectancy was 25–35 yrs outside Europe, and 40 yrs across Western Europe. Today, life expectancy is 60–70 yrs "in most countries." Our world is not perfect, but it is improving. Those who wax lyrical about 'the good old days' have got it wrong. There was never anything good about rickets, polio, illiteracy, tenements, work–houses, debtors' prisons, geographical immobility, bigotry, racism, eugenics, sexism, homophobia and religionism – discrimination on the basis of religion or religious beliefs. Now *that* was a bad world.

**Dr Simon Bennett**

Director
Civil Safety and Security Unit
University of Leicester
Leicester, UK

# Introduction

Rajinder S. Jutla, Ph.D.

For those of us interested in the future of North American cities, this book offers a clear–eyed overview of the complex issues facing them. With increasing population, our cities are forced to deal with many new challenges, such as global warming, urban congestion, and crime. All these issues are tied to our political, social and economic systems, so to address them, we need to have a well–defined interdisciplinary approach to planning which has an input of multiple variables.

Dr. Bonner exposes readers to the complexity of urban issues in a very simple, readable and understandable manner. He provides new ideas, outside the box, for planning our cities. Some of them include to "pop up," "clip on" and "grow out" – building onto the water in our cities to help make them more livable, efficient and safe. His conceptual discussion for the development of floating cities is very interesting. A Japanese company is already developing plans for a floating city to save the Pacific island nation from rising sea levels. He emphasizes the importance of waterways to be developed as efficient highways for transporting people and material, and further explores how shorelines can be used for more than just beaches and boat yards. According to Dr. Bonner we need to plan our cities based on not only human behavior but also the natural surroundings.

As the title suggests, the book emphasizes the need for cities to develop an evacuation or emergency plan to ensure the safety of its residents in case of disaster, caused by either unpredictable weather or by human error. Natural disasters due to bad weather, hurricanes, and tornados are common on the East coast of the United States and the Midwest. Human error disaster stems from problems like leakage from nuclear reactors. Many cities unfortunately are devoid of this kind of planning. Dr. Bonner also points out the need for planners to elicit participation from residents in the planning process since the number of people affected by such plans is much greater than those doing the planning. In conclusion, he suggests a seven step approach to deal with this complex issue of providing safety to people in cities.

The book is full of new ideas and covers a wide range of topics. It is an excellent treatise of North American cities and will help citizens understand the problems and challenges facing them. I would recommend this as essential reading for everyone interested in emerging urban issues as well as students of urban geography, urban planning, architecture and design.

**Rajinder S. Jutla, Ph.D.**

Professor and Director of Planning Program
Department of Geography, Geology & Planning
Missouri State University

# Beginnings

I consider myself to be one of the lucky ones of the earth's billions. I can look back on a childhood that was, if not idyllic, then certainly warm, safe, and comforting.

In my mind's eye, I can see our neat suburban home with its little plot of land from which my parents cleared the weeds, so they could plant flowers. The neighbours did the same and informally competed for the best lawns and rock gardens. I can recall sitting with my father by a newly planted tree. He told me that one day in the future that tree would provide me with shelter from the sun. It was a comforting thought for a five-year-old.

However, it wasn't long before I realized that my comfortable and safe little world seemed to need constant attention. My mother was always busy cleaning, cooking or gardening while my father would mow the grass or deal with projects and problems in the basement or attic. As I grew older, I realized this constant attention wasn't confined to my home but extended to the area around it. The streets needed to be fixed, sidewalks had to be repaired, storm drains had to be cleared of leaves, and trees had to be trimmed so they didn't interfere with power lines. All this effort, I realized, helped make my world efficient and safe.

Today, I live in a city with a population far more concentrated than an old typical suburb. I live right downtown and I have for years. I'm in a high-rise with no lawn to mow or snow to shovel. I wonder if my neighbours' children will grow up to enjoy the same cozy, comfortable, childhood memories I have. My city has long prided itself on being one of the best-run large cities in North America. Like all large urban areas it attracts a steady stream of new residents, placing its infrastructure, public services, amenities and governance under constant stress. Worse, its rate of growth appears to have outstripped its ability to respond to some of its most critical challenges – such as transport.

In 2008 our world passed a significant milestone. For the first time in history more than half the world's population was living in urban areas. The World Health Organization estimates that by 2050 almost three–quarters of the Earth's population of 9.3 billion humans will live in cities. Hollywood has already churned out several movies with apocalyptic visions of this urbanized future.

I don't think we need to be afraid of a big city future.

To many people, particularly in North America, small town and country living represents a golden age of cultural cohesion and social values. Big city living brought urban blight, environmental challenges, congestion and crime. It turns out, however, that large urban areas are much more efficient at delivering quality services to their residents than are rural communities. Big cities in the developed world also happen to be economic engines in their own right. They create wealth, which is why people want to move there.

Obviously some cities are more successful than others and economic success, by itself, is not enough. However, big cities have been around long enough for us to have been able to study them and see what we can learn so that we can head off some of the problems we know are coming our way. I suspect the biggest problem we will face is that of inaction – not due to laziness, but to indecision, as we commission study after study in search of the perfect solution and then argue over how we pay for it.

If we really want our cities to be able to cope with the challenges posed by ever increasing populations we may have to change the way we plan. Hoping for long–term solutions is attractive, but is it practical when we know the challenges we face tomorrow may be very different from the ones we face today?

Perhaps we should pay more attention to re–evaluating our natural surroundings to see how we can incorporate them into making our cities more efficient and safe. For example, many cities border on sizable bodies of water that provide recreational opportunities when the weather is mild – but also cause concerns about flooding of low lying areas when the weather is bad. Yet waterways can be as efficient as highways in transporting people and material, and shorelines can be used for more than just beaches and boat yards. The construction industry has adopted a modular approach that allows it greater flexibility with projects. Perhaps we need to adopt a modular approach to big city planning so that we can be more flexible in dealing with growth and changing needs.

If we want our cities to be a source of inspiration rather than unmanageable problems the time to start thinking about how we deal seriously with change is now. I hope this book helps point the way towards more efficient, comfortable and primarily safer cities in the years to come. Safe streets and neighbourhoods are important, but even a cursory review of news reports from the around the world shows hardly anywhere is completely free from the risk of disaster, either natural or those caused by human behaviour or misbehaviour. For that reason I have included a section examining how we might plan for the unthinkable:

how do we help people to move safely out of the safe cities we are creating if – and when – disaster strikes?

In North America we have become quite familiar with the annual disruptions to life in regions that experience hurricanes, tornadoes, floods, ice storms or forest fires. However, Hurricanes Katrina and Rita and Superstorm Sandy showed us just how unprepared we are to deal with 'The Big One.' Nearly all communities have emergency plans drawn up to maintain essential services and keep people safe. Of course we don't know if they'll work until disaster strikes and they get put into practice – but then it will be too late to make corrections. So I decided to undertake a reality check.

I selected 100 cities in the developed and English–speaking world and asked to study their emergency preparedness plans. Not surprisingly I found a huge range in the approaches taken and solutions offered. In general, though, I am not convinced that those given the task of preparing these plans have come to grips with the extent and magnitude of the problems they may confront. All too often clear instructions in plain language were avoided in favour of bureaucratic jargon sprinkled liberally with baffling acronyms. I've included an appendix in which I rank the cities according to the efficiency, accessibility, accountability and other key attributes of their emergency plans.

We can only hope these plans will never be needed. However, simply waiting to find out if they will work, or fail, is not much of a choice.

Allan Bonner,
Faculty Club,
University Of Toronto

*A triumph both of technology and civic vision, the Space Needle has become a global symbol of Seattle.*

# Caution:
# Mistakes will be made!

I't's astounding how wrong we all can be most of the time. We all know it and yet we somehow assume that when the 'experts' put their heads together to come up with solutions to our urban problems, big or small, they are going to get it right.

The evidence says otherwise.

Was Le Corbusier really serious when in the early 1920s he proposed radical changes to architecture as a way of preventing revolution and class warfare? Lucio Costa and Oscar Niemeyer may have hoped they were advancing a classless society when they collaborated on building Brasilia from scratch in the late 1950s. But the spacious capital city they created is populated by politicians, diplomats and government bureaucrats. Ordinary people, including those who provide the city's services, live in nearby satellite cities that are nowhere near as grand.

Even Frank Lloyd Wright was criticized for helping to spread, rather than contain, suburbia. Herbert Muschanp, the architecture critic for the *New York Times* from 1992 to 2004 wrote:

> *"....the greatest architect of all time had made possible the conversion of America's natural paradise to an asphalt continent of Holiday Inns, Tastee–Freeze stands, automobile graveyards, billboards, smog, tract housing, mortgaged and franchised coast to coast."*

Regardless, the best example I have of the propensity to be wrong is a pedestrian one – in more ways than one. Incorrect design and the hubris of designers are brought home every time I see a well–worn path through a landscaped area.

Pedestrians are voting with their feet to avoid the planned pathways in favour of their own routes.

Despite all evidence that we have a higher probability of being wrong than right, we seem to assume that others are more right than wrong. Why else would the world emulate the car orientation of Los Angeles decades after problems began? Why would Toronto's Spadina Expressway (now the Allen Road) and Montreal's Decarie Expressway look suspiciously like the Cross–Bronx Expressway? Why would public housing in Toronto's Regent Park look like a smaller version of federally funded public housing projects in New York and other American cities? We emulate what's being done in the big city. We all want to drink from the cup of modernity – even if we know there's a good chance we'll have a hangover.

Nevertheless, there are examples of planners getting it right. Two that I know of happen to be in Canada. Around the turn of the 20th century, civic leaders were convinced that Winnipeg was going to be the Chicago of Canada, with a population to match. They installed a gravity fed system to deliver fresh water from Lake of the Woods, 150 kilometres to the southeast that has served the city to this day. Winnipeg's population never did match Chicago's, but the pipeline has been extended 200 kilometres to the west to also serve the city of Brandon.

My first home in Toronto was in the borough of East York. While the main street, Danforth Avenue, consisted mainly of low–density retail stores we had a subway line to take us into downtown. This was a result of civic foresight. While building the Bloor–Danforth viaduct over the Rosedale Ravine, 100 years ago, planners included a lower deck for rail traffic. It was almost 50 years later when subway trains began to use those tracks!

Great American examples come from cities at the opposite ends of the population spectrum. In Seattle, some civic boosters wanted the theme for the 1962 World's Fair to be "The Festival of the West." Just imagine the city's image if the fair's lasting legacy was a permanent rodeo rather than its Space Needle and monorail. It was smart to focus on high–technology and the future. Was this a legacy of Boeing's history in Seattle? Did the focus of the fair and tradition in Seattle help motivate Bill Gates? Who knows for sure, but the Seattle fair and its legacy of modernity was surely of greater value than a cowboy motif in a city not really known for cowboys.

The Space Needle was actually a victory within a victory. Edward E. Carlson, Chair of the 1962 fair, famously drew his vision of the Space Needle on a napkin. But time was running out and he had to scramble to find investors. Finally, a month after the deadline to begin construction, he got his financing in order, finished the project on time and it became one of the great civic symbols of the world. As a footnote, it retired its debt in just 18 months, proving that some big ideas actually make money.

New York City is also the beneficiary of some accidental good planning. The cable car or tram to Roosevelt Island was a temporary solution to the problem of having no bridge to the island. Today, it remains an unusual and fun means of urban transport at 59th Street. High Line Park exists because even though the city had plans to demolish this abandoned, elevated railway it didn't have the money to proceed. Meanwhile, community activists came up with their own plans. Now it's a unique urban park, invigorating the third floors of many buildings, raising real estate values and creating interesting dining and other areas underneath its structure.

And then there's the legacy of Robert Moses, the man who did more to shape New York City in the middle of the 20th century than anyone else, even though he wasn't an architect, engineer or trained planner and never held an elected office. But he made himself indispensable to several New York mayors and with their political support he got things done.

When he arrived at a Depression–era works project to find able–bodied men sawing the handles off shovels to burn them in barrels to keep warm, Moses put them to work using complete shovels. On another occasion he hired hundreds of architects for a public project. Then he announced that there would be cots set up in the hallways for sleeping and that anyone who went home at the end of the day need not come back. When it came time to refurbish the much neglected Central Park Zoo, he did so 24 hours a day, seven days a week until it was done.

However, his most productive years came after World

*The Roosevelt Island tram in Manhattan on a foggy morning.*

War II when the American Housing Act of 1949 established a federally-subsidized program to help cities with slum clearance programs and urban renewal projects, including public housing. Moses built more public housing projects and expressways than most other cities combined, simply because he had plans ready to go. He also built a dozen giant swimming pools for 50,000 bathers, hundreds of playgrounds, dozens of parks, and closed the deal to establish the head-quarters of the United Nations in New York over a weekend.

Yet he had his detractors. He acknowledged favouring the automobile over public transit "because we live in a motorized age," and was more interested in grandiose plans for expressways and tower blocks than in preserving long–established neighbourhoods. By the mid–1950s his block–busting approach to redevelopment ran into opposition from a new generation of city planners as well as community activists, including Jane Jacobs, author of "The Death and Life of American Cities" – a book that reflected their concerns.

After battling successfully to stop some of Moses' more extreme plans – one would have driven a four–lane highway through the centre of Washington Square Park, a second would have razed 14 blocks in the heart of Greenwich Village and a third called for an elevated, 10–lane super highway through lower Manhattan – Jane Jacobs moved to Canada and took up residence in Toronto. Within a very short time she took a leading role in a grassroots movement to stop another highway (the Spadina Expressway) as well as a drive to revitalize the King–Spadina area, with which I'm very familiar because it's my former neighbourhood.

Just as Robert Moses was on good terms with a series of mayors of New York, so Jane Jacobs became a favourite of mayors of Toronto. Indeed, at least two of the city's top planners worked with her on her ideas to revitalize my old

neighbourhood. The 'new' King–Spadina called for mixed uses of land. Revitalization brought a welcome influx of condo–dwellers, but we also ended up with about 80 night-clubs. Before long, King–Spadina became about equal to one of Toronto's public housing areas as the most dangerous in Toronto. Some time later I told the city's Commissioner of Planning that I considered this to be "planned violence." He responded: "Sometimes mistakes are made."

It's ironic that two of the biggest names of the planning profession in 20th century North America are remembered because they had diametrically opposed viewpoints – and they weren't even trained planners! Another thing they had in common was that they both made mistakes – including Jane Jacobs' failed attempt at being a developer or gentrifier. But, she's in good company, along with Le Corbusier, Costa, Neimeyer and Frank Lloyd Wright. So, I begin this project of planning for safer cities assuming I'll be wrong at least as often as they were.

But I have a plan to make only small errors, because even if there are errors, small might be beautiful, as least according to British economist E. F. Schumacher. And if the small errors aren't beautiful, they may be removable. This is why I have plans to have things rise up, clip on, and grow out (onto the water) of our cities to help make our cities more liveable, efficient and safe. I like to call it reversible, or forgivable public policy. Even if these initiatives work like a dream, events over time may make them obsolete. But they can then be removed.

# Erasing Mistakes

Cities have developed into complex organisms. They are built of bricks, mortar, wood, concrete, steel and many other materials – but they are occupied by humans. This occupation turns cities into something like an anthill – but without any unity of purpose. If something goes wrong there is no instinct to follow an agreed-upon path to a solution. There are no easy cures for what is ailing many of our cities.

We know many cities are under enormous pressures because of rapid growth, ageing populations and economic turbulence. These contribute to social and cultural problems, increased poverty, ill health and crime. Like Robert Moses and Jane Jacobs, some of us may think we can solve, or at least alleviate, these problems by forward planning for better streets, housing, parks and transport. However, we all need to remember that those who will be affected by these plans are much more numerous than those doing the planning. They need to be involved.

We also know that public hearings and consultations can be cumbersome, time-consuming and – as far as planners, developers and some politicians are concerned – mere obstacles to progress. So how can we speed up the process of trying to improve the conditions of our cities, without taking the risk that we will do more harm than good?

Just imagine that we had the ability to test our ideas cost effectively under actual conditions in real time to see if they worked. If they don't, we erase them and move on. Well, I think we do have that ability. Here are some examples of my reversible and forgivable public policy:

# Popping Up

Sometimes new and interesting amenities in urban areas just seem to pop up. Lawn chairs, pianos and umbrellas in Times Square may be one of the best known examples. There also have been experiments with park benches, picnic tables and even drinking fountains with multiple heads that can attach to fire hydrants that pop up during very hot weather.

Restaurants have been described as businesses whose owners have the opportunity to spend $300,000 to find out in one week that they've picked the wrong location. Pop–ups can combat this. A pop–up restaurant can appear in an empty store front with kitchen facilities, or in a temporary building made of shipping containers on a vacant piece of land so that entrepreneurs can test the market.

*Canada's Sugar Beach is a new park that was built in 2010. It has transformed a surface parking lot in a former industrial area into Toronto's second urban beach at the water's edge.*

In fact pop–up restaurants have been around for many years but they are coming into their own because of the explosion of social media. Recent phenomena such as crowd–funding can raise short–term capital for start up costs to help new chefs gain attention. Customers can track them to their new locations using Twitter or Facebook. One of the strangest locations is in Winnipeg, where a pop–up restaurant appears only in the depths of winter on the ice at the frozen confluence of the Assiniboine and Red rivers.

Retail stores use pop-ups as well. Ralph Lauren famously used tractor–trailer trucks to get his preppy lines of clothing to university and college campuses. Many of

**Muvbox**
*Fold Out Shipping Container. Pop-up facilities can also pop out. This is a fold out shipping container that can serve as a temporary restaurant during festivals. With a little imagination it could also be a health station or career counselling unit installed at schools or in disadvantaged neighbourhoods. In emergencies, such as a power outage, hot dog carts, chip wagons and these facilities can feed neighbourhoods for a few days.*

these campuses, like Shakespeare's 'green world', were in small communities with limited retail outlets. Cutting out distributors may have also appealed to Lauren, but regardless, his retail outlet popped up in a truck and disappeared after serving his customers. New lines of clothing, discount items and new designers can all be featured in pop up locations, including prefabricated ones and existing, underused facilities.

can be as simple as a basement apartment with its own separate entrance, or two–storey additions built alongside or behind the host building, depending on the space available. Vancouver permits such extensions in lanes and backyards. The advantage is that when this extra space is not required by the owners for their families it can be rented. These 'clip–ons' can help increase population density – and also help accommodate our ageing populations.

## Clipping On

We've become accustomed to seeing cities expanding by adding suburbs or by building higher apartment buildings and condominium towers. Perhaps we can also look at simpler methods that don't require such huge outlays of money and effort. We already add decks, rec rooms, roof terraces and granny flats. Perhaps we should take this a bit further. One idea is the expandable home. Homes can expand by taking over part, or all, of the space of another. They can 'clip–on' extra room as their needs and families grow, then 'clip–off' as their requirements change.

A version of expandable homes is already evident in Canada (and probably elsewhere). Asians, in particular, don't like the idea of sending their aged parents to live in old folks' homes. So they are working with architects to adapt their homes so they will be able to accommodate their parents, without actually living together. The solution

*Container City 2*
*Leamouth England. Containers used on ships and trucks can be given a second life as 'pop-up' facilities in urban areas. They can be installed quickly without disrupting neighbourhoods and removed if the use turns out to be less popular than thought. Multiple units can be stacked to form elaborate retail and housing structures.*

# Going Out

For hundreds of years our transport system was our waterways. Our population centres are on water because people who settled there could trade, travel and receive visitors. In living memory, Canadians could get almost half–way into the continent on a 'boat–train.' They boarded a train in downtown Toronto, which took them to Collingwood where they boarded a ship, which traveled to Thunder Bay. Anyone who has driven from the east into Manitoba in Canada or the Dakotas in the US knows how welcome using this waterway would be. The use of our internal and coastal waterways for long–distance travel may not be a realistic dream, but it is time to go back out onto the water for some of our local travel, recreational, and other needs.

In my mother's day, she lived on the water – in Toronto. She speaks of long summers and long summer days spent on the beach just south of her home at Leslie and Queen Streets – an area called The Beach. She speaks of ferry rides to dances along the shore – at Sunnyside and as far away as Port Dalhousie on the Niagra Peninsula. Pleasure trips in

***Spirit of America***
*Staten Island Ferry. Many of our cities abut water – our original transport system. It's a wonder we don't use commuter ferries more. They also provide evacuation capacity and a tourist attraction. They can be rented for convention visitors as well.*

The Edmonton Queen River-boat offers a unique way to relax, have dinner, hold events and get married. The boat travels up and down the North Saskatchewan River, offering guests fine dining and a picturesque backdrop.

other cities – up the Hudson from New York, up and down the Mississippi and along our west coast – were common.

Going out in this context is going out on the water to live, work and play. The reversible aspect of this plan is that if the water gets rough, we can come back in. If it gets too cold or if the water freezes, we can make going out a seasonal activity. Within the context of safety, if it's a little costly to use our waterways, we may be rewarded during an emergency, but if not, we only suffer the incremental cost.

So let's take a look at what opportunities our oceans, lakes and rivers have to offer.

# Waterways and the Case for Floating Technology

Our history in North America is tied closely to water. When our forests were too dense to pass through, the lakes and rivers were our transport systems. Settlement occurred along these systems to ensure that as many people as possible had access to water. Today our waterfronts seem more like barriers. Perhaps we can change our views and again look to our waterways to help solve some of today's urban problems.

There is often a clash when it comes to finding ways for land uses and human activities to co–exist. Airports and their neighbours squabble over noise and pollution, with a negative effect on business, on taxes paid and thus on available funds for social purposes. Negotiations over

how to revitalize social housing and neighbourhood amenities causes delays. Residents organize to oppose infill towers because of height or density. Citizens oppose industry in their backyards. Many people in my current neighbourhood, Liberty Village, oppose diesel–driven trains running parallel to the clogged Gardiner Expressway where slow–moving cars and trucks emit more exhaust than they would if there were fewer vehicles on that road. Ironically, there might be fewer vehicles on that road if some of the drivers were riding the diesel train.

There is ample evidence of friction among people who have different visions of appropriate uses of land. However, if there were more land, perhaps there would be fewer squabbles and, as it happens, floating technology can create

*Opposite: Sitting just offshore, these floating ecopolises could serve as homes for former shore residents of urban cities as waters rise due to global warming.*

31

more 'land.' The technology already is used for airstrips in Japan and for the offshore oil industry around the world.

This option would allow communities to locate industry, housing and amenities in the waterways that abut the densest parts of cities. Since each would be purpose–built, environmental and other concerns could be addressed more quickly and completely than with traditional structures on land.

The natural wave action buffeting the facility could be harnessed as a power supply, as could solar energy and the entire structure could become a fish–friendly habitat. Remediation at the end of the life of the facility would also be easier. Population shifts and changing needs could be met with a literal shift of the floating facility to a new neighbourhood where parks, schools, jobs or housing might be needed – or to a remote location for repairs.

# Manufacturing

There may have been a time when industry co-existed with other land uses more harmoniously than it does today. It may have been that industrialists such as August Thyssen and his family members quite enjoyed living in the smoke and noise of the world's first successful effort at corporate integration. Perhaps the workers in his mines and factories appreciated living beside the furnaces and smoke stacks belching flames and smoke because it raised their living standards – and they didn't have complete information about the ill–effects of pollution.

Today we know better. The smokestacks almost certainly will have scrubbers and point of impingement monitors to reduce pollution. Even so, we are in a public policy environment in which years of public meetings, regulatory hearings and legislative approvals may be needed to start up a manufacturing concern. Excluding nuclear, chemical or military uses, citizens do not normally mobilize to oppose a manufacturing or industrial plant dozens of miles away. They are more likely to mobilize to protect their own backyards.

What if a manufacturing concern were out of sight, out of mind and environmentally friendly? The latter is the perhaps the most important point and floating technology may be an excellent way of achieving

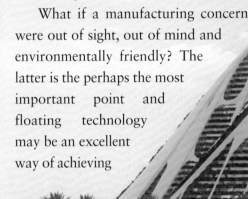

*Moving along with the ocean currents, these adaptable ecocities would be capable of moving close to shore for repairs, resupply or to facilitate trade with terrestrial cities.*

an environmentally sustainable end without generating intense stakeholder opposition. By definition, a floating facility has no neighbours. There may be people within sight of it. There will be people living, working, learning and playing on the adjacent land. But there could be hundreds of metres or even several kilometres between the floating factory and its nearest neighbours.

More importantly, a floating facility purpose–built for industrial use could avoid many of the challenges facing land–based concerns trying to locate on a greenfield or brownfield site. One of the frustrations of cleaning up a brownfield site is that it is often adjacent to another brownfield site. When the first site is cleaned, pollutants immediately begin leaching from the neighbouring dirty site onto the newly cleaned one. However, this problem won't exist for a floating facility. When a floating factory comes to the end of its useful life, it can be towed back to port where it can be safely cleaned and broken up for salvage.

*When at sea, the lilypad's central lagoon stabilizes the ecopolis and supplies a fresh water source as it travels on the water all over the world.*

# Low–Cost Housing

In mature cities, we struggle with where to put low–cost housing. Many of the economic inputs are relatively inflexible – services, land, labour and materials. There can be economies of scale and creative use of density transfers. There has been co-op building in the past with neighbours having working bees to get single–family homes built. Site–specific labour agreements and LEED (Leadership in Energy and Environmental Design) techniques, which include the re–use of materials can also achieve savings, but perhaps only on the margins. We need to keep seeking more ways to make more housing more affordable.

The type of housing that needs to be more affordable is an important question. On the surface, we appear to have had about sixty years of public policy designed to foster home ownership and improve existing housing stock. Ultimately, this seems to be an assistance program for those who are already well–off enough to have a home or close to having the resources to acquire a home. It may be that all boats rise with a rising tide and that improving existing housing stock has a positive effect on supply and demand. It may also be that a policy which turns some renters into home owners creates an aspiration in the renter population and a sense of accomplishment in the new home owners. This may cause both groups to feel they have a greater stake in society. It may also be that even

those who can't aspire to home ownership at least feel that the economic and societal system in which we are operating does work for most people and may someday work better for them. Thus, it is possible that this public policy has had a calming effect on a population that might otherwise vent frustrations in unproductive ways.

Even if this theory of home ownership as an opiate is correct, this public policy leaves out those for whom there is little or no housing and no hope of housing. These are the people with substance abuse issues, mental health issues, and serious economic issues. There are inadequate numbers of housing units available for them. There is an extra challenge for children, women, and aboriginals. These are fast-growing groups of homeless people with additional battles of discrimination and power imbalance

*Houseboats in Amsterdam. Houseboats are an easy way to enliven our waterways. Shorelines and inlets can become vibrant almost overnight and can serve as unique bed and breakfast accommodation for visitors. Even if these are only occupied seasonally, they can be a manifestation of the long–accepted notion that noise, people and light keep neighbourhoods safe.*

*A collection of amphibious auto–sufficient cities at sea near the flooded atolls where residents used to live.*

to fight. However, a first step is to generate a supply of low–cost rental housing units and remain vigilant for remedies to the other barriers to housing that certain groups face. Low–cost units might need to be configured to allow for counselling, security, day–care, schooling, skills–training, healing lodges, elder counselling and other culturally–sensitive amenities.

Dedicated facilities can be prone to stigmatization. Public policy makers need to guard against this, while also guarding against forced–mixed use with dangerous industrial uses next to day–care centres. A floating facility might present several opportunities to achieve an equitable balance.

The first role for a floating facility might be in the manufacturing of homes and the components of homes. For decades there has been a dream that prefabrication and modularization might be an answer to the high cost of construction. One can purchase a variety of kitchen and bathroom cabinets, ready to install, but not an entire kitchen or bathroom. There was a time when some predicted that an old kitchen or bathroom could be fork–lifted out of a home and a new one installed in a day, but this has not come to pass.

There has been progress in the prefabrication of entire single–family homes. Various manufacturers make and partially assemble conventional looking, three–bedroom homes for transport by truck to a building site. Some of these homes are transported as a single unit. Sometimes the components are numerous and sometimes the homes are in two halves.

A floating facility could make components for housing such as trusses, joists, cabinets, entire rooms or fully–finished 400–600 square foot granny flats, mobile homes and modular homes. Components could be packaged on the facility, or assembled and then lifted by crane onto barges or trucks for either ground or water transport. Containers could be lifted onto railroad cars if the floating facility were towed to a location along the lake close to railroad tracks.

## Less Impact on Communities

It's common for urban and infrastructure renewal projects to disturb and disrupt nearby communities. Neighbourhood and planning meetings were acrimonious in New York during Robert Moses' urban renewal projects. All cities have experienced versions of these tensions.

One way to address some of these problems is with off–site construction facilities. Components could then be transported to the site and installed with less disruption. Precast and pre–stressed concrete, railroad ties, carbon fibre sono–tubes filled with concrete and installed on site as pylons on which to construct a building, monorail or bridge are just some of the possible applications. If the noisy, dusty and awkward work were done off–site on a floating facility, it would be less disruptive to traffic, businesses and residents. When a project is finished, the floating facility would move to a new location where it's needed.

Moving cargo by water or rail is less disruptive than by truck, especially if the truck is driving through city streets. There is less environmental impact and fuel used when heavy cargoes are moved by water as well. Here again, if demographics change and a community begins shrinking or has changing needs, some of the modular housing and even infrastructure could be uninstalled and shipped to a new location – by water.

Renewal of infrastructure is one thing, but renewal of housing stock, particularly public or social housing, can be harrowing for those about to be displaced. In Toronto, we have two social housing sites that will be demolished and then re–built. Because one of these projects, Regent Park, is fairly close to the lakeshore an option might be to move residents into temporary floating accommodation nearby so they could still use the services they are used to: Shopping, schools, health and recreation centres. That way their sense of dislocation would be lessened.

If an emerging or changing neighbourhood needs a service such as a food store, fitness centre, police station, health centre or other amenity, one can be provided easily

on a floating facility nearby. When entrepreneurs, zoning and planning catch up to the community's needs, the floating facility could be moved easily. If a community loses certain services or critical mass, the floating facility could address these changes. If there is insufficient competition or sensitivity to a community's needs, corporations with a mature sense of corporate social responsibility could provide a counter balance. Floating facilities could provide temporary community amenities as needed.

**Oasis of the Seas**
*Floating City. This floating facility could house a concert hall, sports stadium, hospital or other needed civic amenities. When neighbourhoods change and needs evolve, new facilities could be towed into place. These facilities could include police, fire, EMS, grocery stores and housing. When no longer needed, there'd be no need for demolition as was the case with Seattle's Kingdome or St. Louis' Pruitt Igoe housing project.*

37

# Parks and Recreation

Dissatisfaction with urban neighbourhoods often focuses on poor quality or non–existent housing and inadequate amenities. Even in a relatively well–off area such as the former East York in what is now Toronto, a major civic initiative involved buying houses as they became available in order to create mini–parks. On a larger scale, many cities have 'fresh air funds' which are charitable initiatives to get disadvantaged children out of the city and into green space. A floating facility could be towed into place each summer and used for this same purpose.

These facilities could be adapted quite easily to meet different needs or social changes. When the World Cup draws attention to soccer, pitches could be towed to several locations for young people who want to emulate the sport they see on television. These could easily be turned into football or baseball fields as the situation warrants. The success of natural ice–skating surfaces on the Rideau Canal in Ottawa, Wascana Park in Regina and even occasionally Burnaby Lake in suburban Vancouver (when weather permits), shows that cities that abut suitable waterways could benefit from floating ice–rinks that could be artificially cooled for a longer season.

Different cities will have different preferences and needs. New Yorkers favour asphalt basketball courts. Floating basketball courts moored in the Hudson River might free up some urban space for more traditional green spaces on shore. There could even be floating lacrosse fields in Vancouver and Jai alai courts in Miami.

Some urban areas are becoming dense enough to have differing weather and environmental conditions in different neighbourhoods. Cities themselves have different weather and temperatures than the surrounding open spaces because of the heat retained by concrete and because of other factors. The configuration of high–rise buildings can create pockets of higher temperatures and

*This floating 'air garden' is a relaxing space filled with plants and trees oriented towards a central stage – an ideal setting for debates and discussions around our current ecological challenges.*

elevated air pollution as well. Dark building treatments can add to the problem. Environmental racism suggests that some of the worst polluted urban neighbourhoods correlate with residents of colour. The use of puffers by school children suffering from asthma, made worse by pollution, is a political issue in New York and other cities.

It may be hard to retrofit some of our neighbourhoods to address these issues. Trees and green space might be added. Rooftops can be grassed or painted light colours. But a floating facility might be a quick and less costly way to provide services to neighbourhoods which have these environmental challenges. The installation of grass and trees along the shoreline may cool and clean the air, and provide a facility on which families can walk, picnic and play.

*Basking the glow of the moon, this floating garden serves as both a laboratory and collaborative space promoting waterway restoration.*

**The Float at Marina Bay – Singapore.**
*Floating fields can be towed into place for special games, entertainment events or when the local school is in the championship. Reminiscent of Long Island's Jones Beach, the facility pictured is also a popular concert venue in Singapore.*

school, community or post–secondary institution quickly and cheaply. The facility could morph from one use to another or add uses as the community's needs and preferences changed. The speed would be a result of prefabrication in a remote location to avoid disruption. The cost–saving could result from the facility being adapted or moved when needs change.

There could be similar positive approaches to health and wellness. Line ups for winter flu shots and longer lines for swine flu or other unusual shots might be shorter with dedicated floating facilities. When the seasonal or specific need has passed, the facility could take on a new role. Similarly, the use of hospital emergency rooms as drop-in clinics is costly. Perhaps floating clinics could take the pressure off hospitals. Neighbourhoods with specific demographic needs could be served by public health nurses, health practitioners, geriatric specialists or those with religious and cultural sensitivities.

There are other neighbourhood amenities that a floating facility could provide. Libraries are one example. There seems to be a regular ebb and flow in the need for larger libraries, satellite libraries, bookmobiles, school libraries and so on, in many communities. Public policy does not seem to have evolved to coordinate budgets and activities by two or more government departments or levels of government. Regardless of the administrative challenges, a floating facility could be turned into a library to support a

# Special Needs Amenities

Our population is ageing. This alone will present special housing, health care, dietary and other needs. The growing numbers of women and children who are homeless or in sub–standard housing present other special challenges. There are several million disabled American veterans in the US who also have special needs.

Floating factories could be built in order to provide special needs facilities close to where they are most required. These amenities include access ramps, wider doors, lower and larger doorknobs, grip bars and so on.

Cities on waterways could have floating recreational areas that are especially safe so that grandparents with mobility challenges can be confident when spending time with youngsters. They could have flower and herb gardens easily

*The 'fire garden' is a unique waterline lounge in a floating garden and features relaxing armchairs, a crackling fire and displays on aquatic life that will engage visitors.*

accessible to people in wheelchairs. They could be specially designed so that those with impaired vision would be able to hear those moving around them, and the hearing impaired could clearly view their surroundings.

Students have need for specific types of housing. They need low–cost housing near their post–secondary institutions and many of those institutions are close to water. Floating facilities might serve them well. Students, especially single students, can tolerate smaller units and higher density than many other demographic groups. Students generally have a seasonal need for housing that coincides with the school years. Having such units to serve students can free up existing market units for others.

There is a saying predicting that a community without low–cost housing will be a community with very few artists. Artists are not the most disadvantaged of groups. But artists add to a community and their presence should be encouraged. A floating facility might provide low–cost and transient housing for artists. It might also contain studios, rehearsal space, space for educational activities and community performance halls. These facilities could be shared with fine arts and other students. Artscape is a not–for–profit, urban development organization that is making progress in the provision of studio and living space at reduced cost to artists, which might find using floating facilities effective. In summer months, if not needed, the facility could be towed to other lake front communities for use by their local artists.

## Short–term Industrial Needs

Since the start of the century, Toronto has experienced a building boom that shows no signs of ending or slowing down. Most new buildings are condominiums. Yet there is a shortage of skilled workers who are familiar with the American Society of Mechanical Engineers' (ASME) code, heat–loss calculations, degree days, and maintaining and retrofitting for energy conservation, as well as other important technical matters.

It could be that in the life of a city there comes a time when certain skills are required and certain activities present unique opportunities to learn on the job. Perhaps in this case, a floating facility could serve a special educational need. There could be a partnership among building management companies, Trent University's Environmental Centre of Knowledge in nearby Peterborough, unions and professional engineering societies. They could offer a training program just a short walk from many of the construction sites and even be moved along the lake shore among different areas of construction, as needed. The students could be housed on the facility as part of a practicum featuring both classroom instruction and on the job training on construction sites and in finished buildings. When the need for training has been satisfied or the building boom over, the facility could be moved near a number of community colleges and universities near the lake to provide temporary housing or other services.

There may be also a wider industrial application for floating facilities. North American industrial workers have not made a final, collective decision on their attitudes towards overtime work. In Germany and many parts of Europe, it is considered antisocial, robbing families of time with the worker. In some North American enterprises workers consider overtime part of their remuneration package and a necessity to maintain their lifestyles. Overtime has been a contentious issue in auto worker negotiations with the union hesitant to give management carte blanche to call workers in during off–hours.

There may be an approach to short–term demand for industrial and other workers that a floating facility can address. If the auto workers' union co–sponsored a residential floating facility that could be moored near production facilities in Oakville or Oshawa as needed, it could support temporary workers for the nearby plant. The workers might be single, retired or have personal reasons for being willing to work extra hours. There might also be workers who can only work half–shifts because of age or other issues, and the floating facility could make it easier to share shifts. The facility might contain child–care and other amenities that support the workers' families. If the car manufacturer took a large order for taxis or delivery vans, it could be sure of on–time delivery through the efforts of these workers. The ability to work three shifts per day, seven days per week with workers who were willing to do so with minimal disruption of family life could be a unique selling feature for plants near the water.

*This 'water' garden serves as the main entrance to the floating garden. With a glass floor that showcases the river below, this reception area is ideal for temporary exhibitions on ecological issues.*

# Waste Management

People do not want a waste management facility in their backyards. Trucks present conventional traffic problems and noise. Odours may signal emissions that cause ill-health. Burning for energy at least captures some of the value in waste, but this is a high-technology activity which can release endocrine disruptors, dioxins and furans if not done within a specified range of temperatures. Even composting can leave residues of plastic and metal, which pose a danger to farm animals if the organic material is used to nourish farm fields.

Trucking waste long distances may prevent local neighbourhood disputes. There may be a dump located in a neighbouring jurisdiction that welcomes waste. But, there's no free lunch. Trucks pose a structural threat to highways, exacerbated by the use of radial tires, uneven or improper tire pressure, uneven loads and other factors. Moreover, with about 50,000 highway deaths each year in North America, adding the trucking of garbage to our roads obviously poses a greater risk to human health than dealing with our garbage in the community that generated the waste. But then we're back to neighbourhood disputes over the use of land for waste management. Perhaps floating technology could help resolve this dilemma.

A floating facility could be towed, pushed by tugboat or driven under its own power to major collection points along the waterway. In Greater Toronto, there could be a regular schedule for waste collection at pick-up points along the lake shore from Oakville to Oshawa.

The waste could be hand-sorted, as is done in several European cities. Reusable materials could be sold, swapped or given away at community street events. Organic matter could be off-loaded to another floating facility for composting and delivery to ports around the lake for farm and gardening use. Recyclable metals and plastics could be dealt with in other floating facilities. Combustible material could be burned in a power-generating facility that plugs into the power grid in sparsely populated ports around the lake. Finally, waste that would normally go into landfill could be put in a secure, lined, concrete floating landfill site that uses and reuses leachate in a bio reactor to speed up the decomposition and might even capture methane or heat energy from the process.

These uses would not be without their critics. No doubt all can agree on the need to reduce our waste as a first step, reuse what we can and recycle what we can. But even reuse and recycling efforts need a physical space to achieve these ends. Regardless of our success in these areas, there will still be some waste that has to be dealt with through burning, landfill or other traditional means. Even ash left over from burning has to go somewhere. However, handling waste on a floating facility may reduce public apprehension and opposition.

# Deliver the Goods

I can't think of any major city that isn't plagued by delivery vehicles of all sizes trying to manoeuvre through congested streets at all hours of the day to deliver the food and less vital consumer products we all find necessary to our urban existence. It's as if our entire lives come wrapped in paper, plastic, cardboard or styrofoam – and sometimes in all of these. In most cases the wrapping is many times bulkier than the product.

There doesn't seem to be any easy way of reducing the amount of waste to be collected and taken away. However, in addition to using floating technology to deal with our mountains of waste, perhaps we could also reduce the traffic congestion caused by so many delivery vehicles. It may be that a floating facility could be used to stockpile goods that a city needs and smaller vehicles could then be used to distribute them with less disruption to neighbourhoods and the environment. It might even be that a floating facility could be laden with produce from smaller communities along the lake shore and, when moored, perform as a farmers' market where city dwellers can access the produce.

*Rendering Freedom*
*Modular Floating City. Our port lands are now more valuable as redeveloped sites for condos and attractions. We can still bring in freight and any cargo to our cities via floating facilities just off the shoreline. The structures on stilts may be more resilient in weather events.*

# Culture

For at least 50 years there have been struggles to make culture more assessable in urban areas. One of New York Park Commissioner Robert Moses' biggest battles was over free performances of Shakespeare plays in Central Park. In 1959, he demanded the theatre troupe performing the plays charge for admission to pay for damage to the grass. He eventually lost.

Many urban areas feature summer productions in parks, including in North York's Earl Bales Park and Toronto's High Park. The Madison Mall was an early effort to turn a high traffic street into a pedestrian mall during the Lindsay years in New York City. Also in the 1960s and 1970s, Sparks Street in Ottawa became a permanent mall and Yonge Street in Toronto became a temporary mall during summer months and jazz festivals. New York, San Francisco and Vancouver began holding 'Be–Ins' in their large urban parks.

But even with the best planned and well intentioned civic events, there are still squabbles over competing uses of urban space. Drivers, pedestrians, rollerbladers, walkers and bicyclists compete over finite space. Some businesses praise and others condemn turning a retail street into a mall and have statistics on the impact on sales to back up their arguments. Even those who support malls and jazz festivals sometimes bemoan the noise, drinking and garbage that is left behind.

Floating facilities could serve different purposes for such events. One might serve as a pedestrian mall dedicated to recreation, sampling of the foods of different cultures and so on. Another might contain a bandshell for jazz and other music festivals. The floating quality of the facility could serve as a security measure for events featuring alcohol. Putting these events on a dedicated facility might alleviate squabbles with neighbourhoods which don't feel they benefit from closing streets or staging music festivals.

As is the case with all uses of the floating facilities, the initiative will be reversible. If fashion changes, the facility can be adapted to another use and towed elsewhere. Similarly if tastes change and another community along the shoreline wants to host a music festival, the band shell could be towed to the new host location. It may be that one of the most needed and successful amenities of any city is Jones Beach. The museum and permanent exhibit at the East Bathhouse documents the abjectly inadequate recreational facilities for New Yorkers before this massive complex of beaches, grandstand, boardwalk and games was built on Long Island. It is accessible via buses and a parkway system. Some of the activities have included basketball, pitch and putt golf, archery, shuffleboard and calisthenics. There is no reason why some of these activities couldn't be available on floating facilities, moored at the waterfront of many of our cities.

## I Love a Parade

One of the attractive features of urban life is spectacles. There is enough diversity and population density that we can sustain more than just a rustic fall fair. Big cities have big versions of fall fairs – the Canadian National Exhibition in Toronto, State Fairs in the US and the Pacific National Exhibition in Vancouver. But we also have marathons, malls, jazz festivals, car races and other attractions that require road closures. In Toronto the gay pride parade and Caribana bring hundreds of thousands of visitors to the city, but also create traffic jams for the weekend.

Floating technology could address the dilemma of wanting a variety of events, but not wanting our streets to be unusable a dozen times each year. Jones Beach is a great model which illustrates how entertainment can be enhanced in a waterfront setting. The jazz festival doesn't have to shut down our main street, as it has done in the past. It could he held on a series of floating band shells on our waterfront. Parades and even marathons could use our extensive waterfront park and trail system, and then be diverted into the water on a floating, temporary causeway forming a large loop back to the land. This moveable facility might be in almost continuous operation for the summer season with music, athletics, culture, recreation and parades.

## Emergency Response and Crisis Preparedness

Floating facilities can address the challenges faced during emergencies. They could serve as storage for necessities, medical supplies and emergency shelters. Dual purpose facilities could serve recreation, sporting and cultural needs while also being potential temporary shelters. In the case of an evacuation, the most effective transport may be trains and buses. We need plans to shelter, feed, clothe and minister to those who make their way to facilities in communities along the existing transit lines. Floating facilities containing emergency supplies could be towed to where they are closest to points of need during such an event.

We can also imagine a security component. Why not a floating police station that can be situated where it is most needed during an emergency or during an event such as a parade, mass demonstration or sports event?

## Agriculture

Cities and city dwellers are disconnected from agricultural activities. The physical disconnection presents transport, storage and disposal challenges. The psychological disconnect yields attitudinal challenges and knowledge deficits. The discussion about the merits of methanol as a fuel might be enriched if more urban dwellers saw farm tractors burning diesel fuel to sow crops to grow food to be trucked to facilities which turn that food into fuel, after which the fuel is trucked to gas stations for sale. The discussion about eating locally–grown food with the one hundred mile diet might be enriched if more people saw the full life–cycle cost of growing and transporting food from one hundred miles outside of our cities.

Many of our current ways of feeding cities are unsustainable. We truck food in and truck garbage out. Composting in cities feeds rats and raccoons in large numbers. Community gardens are scarce and difficult to keep tidy. Farmers' markets on parking lots are well attended, but finding space for them will be a greater challenge as parking lots are converted into condominiums and other buildings. Moreover, there is a cost to trucking the produce into the city in small, mainly older trucks which are less fuel efficient than newer models.

Floating facilities could address these challenges in several ways. First, farmers could use the facility to sell their produce. There could be some permanent structure to reduce the burden of weekly set up and removal. The permanent structures could service farmers who sell apples, beef, maple syrup and other foodstuffs in the fall and winter. Another floating facility could also serve as a community garden and demonstration project to illustrate economic and environmental lessons for students. Much

like the Central Park Zoo in New York or Riverdale Farm in Toronto, a floating facility could house mini–model farms for educational purposes.

Yet another facility could provide a simple solution to an urban challenge. There is a serious health challenge becoming evident in modern cities. Diabetes, heart disease and obesity seem to be manifestations of a high–fructose, fast–food diet. Perhaps a floating facility could add some variety and healthy choices for commuters who snack or 'graze' as they move through urban areas. It might also provide temporary food sources for large events such as sports matches or concerts. It might also serve as a portable kitchen making healthy meals for use in schools and in agencies which minister to those in need.

## Airports

The Japanese have had great success with floating airstrips. The stability, wave attenuation and ability to carry a load all bode well for other uses. So, why not a fully functioning floating airport? Such a facility could be installed off the east or west coasts of North America or on the Great Lakes, Lake Winnipeg or elsewhere. The remoteness and ability to lengthen runways would make these facilities compatible with a new generations of environmentally friendly, large and super–sonic aircraft. The airport could be moved to accommodate population shifts. Floating or fixed causeways could connect the airports to mass transit and high–speed inter–urban transit.

A floating causeway could connect to a floating airport, making the convergence of modes of transport a gateway to North America. This infrastructure would play the same role in the 21$^{st}$ century as the port of New York played in the 19$^{th}$. So many immigrants disembarked in New York that the services they required to get settled was a significant portion of the economic activity of the city. As more immigrants arrived, more services were required – feeding a nearly self–sustaining economic system.

What might be imagined for a floating airport and high–speed rail links to the major population and political centres of North America? First, like many Middle East and Asian airports, there could be regular flights 24 hours a day, 7 days a week. With the airport isolated in the lake, there would be few neighbours to complain of noise. With a terror–resistant facility and high–speed rail links, the airport could be the gateway to North America for goods in containers which are then offloaded onto rail for further

*Pelamis Wave Power Sea Snake off the Orkney Islands. Harnessing the power of the sea, each of these slender modulating tubes from Pelamis generates power as the interconnected sections flex when the waves pass over them.*

transport. The airport could also be the gateway for passengers. In Europe passengers use rail to get to cities as far away as 800 or so miles – a trip of a few hours. This means that a floating airport in Lake Ontario could easily serve the major American population centres of the eastern seaboard through to Chicago and the Midwest.

The facility could capture wind and solar power. Even gentle wave action could be harnessed by turbines to generate more electricity. Fish need cool, shaded areas in which to spawn and the facility could be designed with edges that mimic the natural contours of the shorelines of lakes, streams and rivers. A floating airport might be self–sustaining and a net benefit to the environment.

## A Floating Reality Check

On the shore side of cities which are on water, there is only expensive land, limited public sector budgets, lack of coordination among levels of government, cities which are slow to zone or plan to help the incomes of the disadvantaged and a hope that market forces will increase the supply of housing or the incomes of disadvantaged. There is inadequate counselling for substance abuse, mental illness, job skills and other challenges.

In part, floating facilities are worth pondering out of desperation. The shore side of cities also face challenges in transport, pollution and the provision of health, education and other services. Imagining airports, causeways, housing, manufacturing and myriad other facilities on the water illustrates the difficulty we have in continuing to manage and improve facilities on land.

Certainly the use of floating facilities may be a solution. We already use causeways and infill, and floating facilities do present a more environmentally–sustainable alternative. There would need to be appropriate controls on the use of the water ways because covering too much area permanently can adversely affect life below the surface.

But our efforts must also be to make the built forms and life conditions on land equitable and sustainable. Otherwise someone in a future generation of planners may write a paper speculating on the value of facilities floating in the air above congested floating facilities on water. Far fetched? No: There's a patent application in California for just such a hovering airstrip.

# Defining Safety

The safer we get, the more we worry. We are blessed to live in an era of antibiotics, life–saving drugs and miracle surgeries. In my lifetime we have cured polio, transplanted hearts, and developed MRI machines. There are problems for sure: Food safety, highway deaths, drug use and crime. But the statistics show we are living longer, healthier and more productive lives, and yet we worry more. Why?

Our ability to measure risk in smaller and smaller parts per million has not kept pace with our ability to understand these minuscule numbers or do anything about them. Fear is a tyrant. It can motivate – helping to keep us safe when we lock our doors and look both ways crossing the street. Fear can also immobilize, as in the flight or fight response. When we are afraid, the part of our brain that controls instinct takes over to send signals to our muscles – getting us ready to run away or stand and fight.

Entire cities can get gripped in this type of paralyzing fear. People worry about taking a trip through an unsafe neighbourhood. We avoid unsafe locations if possible. Tourists don't flock to unsafe cities. Nor do businesses locate in dangerous places.

'Safety' can include freedom from physical harm, worry, the ill–effects of pollution, crime and congestion. Being safe also means freedom to do things: Be mobile, enjoy entertainment, engage in fitness activities and so on. Workers are more productive in safe working environments, knowing they have health care, pensions and that their families will be looked after in the future. Similarly, social well–being is enhanced in a city where citizens feel safe. People are more likely to interact with and help each other if they can find safe places in which to congregate.

One of the core mandates that politicians and public administrators have is keeping citizens safe. There seems to be agreement from both the left and the right of the political spectrum that defence, integrity of borders, education, health, the environment, crime, and other issues are priorities. People of good will and good intention may differ on how to achieve these core goals. Health care is a good example, with some advocating a one insurer public system, some a public and private mix and still others thinking that multiple private insurers is better. But most agree that health is a high priority and that striving for the improvement of the human condition is an appropriate public policy goal.

One specific way in which we can do that is to improve our ability to protect the personal safety of our citizens. This kind of personal safety can encompass road and highway safety, crime, the food and water supply, health care and so on. It becomes most obvious when cities experience what we call disasters, usually – though not always – 'natural' ones. Some notable examples:

- Hurricane Katrina, which devastated New Orleans in late August 2005, causing the evacuation of most of its residents and the sealing off of large parts of the city – sometimes called quarantine or sheltering in place. More than 1,800 people died and the cost of the damage amounted to more than $80 billion.

- Hurricane Rita, which struck the US gulf coast just three weeks after Katrina. While the number of deaths and damage costs were considerably less, Rita caused the relocation of close to 3 million people, including many of those displaced from New Orleans. It was the largest mass evacuation in American history.

- Hurricane (Superstorm) Sandy, which affected 24 states and four Canadian provinces in October 2012. It was the second costliest hurricane in US history (after Katrina).

- Hurricane (later Tropical Storm) Arthur, the first named storm of the 2014 season which came ashore in Nova Scotia, trapping me in a friend's cottage in Prince Edward Island and hampering my drive through New Brunswick – 300,000 people were without power. I experienced the fallout more than the storm – lineups for gasoline mainly.

Weather events alone should cause many residents of North American cities to ponder their fate. Much of what is currently the downtown areas of many cities on the oceans and Great Lakes of this continent were once underwater. The new land created by silt, garbage, fill, draining and other means may be unstable during severe weather events or in earthquakes. Seismic events can cause liquefaction in this unstable material. Residents should not be surprised if some of these areas are underwater again in the future.

Large areas of Calgary were flooded in 2013, Regina and Winnipeg face regular flood threats, and flooding by Quebec's Saguenay River caused one of Canada's costliest natural disasters. Many of our cities are temporarily paralyzed by snow storms on a regular basis. Eastern Canada (Quebec in particular) experienced a devastating ice storm in 1998 that caused as many as 35 deaths and affected millions of people – resulting in 700,000 insurance claims and losses of about $3 billion.

In some ways it's a mystery why we are so unprepared. How did millions of people come to be living on the floodplains of the Souris River in western Canada and the American Midwest? How can snow and ice paralyze a country that is used to snow and ice? Perhaps we all, civic leaders included, are in the same state of denial found among business travellers who drive on our winter highways without adequate winter clothing or emergency supplies in their cars. Why, though, do the Japanese seem more prepared for earthquakes than North Americans are

for weather events, especially for snowstorms in the upper third of the continent?

In order to understand these questions, it might be useful to probe culture, history, reverence for authority and other issues. But, pragmatically, I am interested in improving safety in my community and want to take some immediate action. I can only hope that any success we have keeping the citizens of Toronto safer might also translate into good public policy in other communities. So, I'll start at the community level in the city that has been my home for more than 30 years.

'Toronto the Good', as it used to be called, has had its share of disasters. In 1954, Hurricane Hazel left 81 dead and four thousand families homeless. In November 1979 a 100–car freight train loaded with volatile chemicals derailed and exploded in the western suburb of Mississauga. There were no fatalities, but the hazards posed by leaked chemicals and gases lead to the evacuation of 200,000 people. It was the largest peacetime evacuation in North America until Hurricane Katrina struck New Orleans. Toronto's outbreak of Severe Acquired Respiratory Syndrome (SARS) made headlines around the world in 2003. Recently we've had floods, power outages and an ice storm.

The SARS outbreak provided us with an opportunity to study pandemic planning. One estimate is that in a pandemic about 30% of the population will be dead, sick or pretending to be sick to avoid actually getting sick. Some others will be staying home to care for sick loved ones.

Some health care workers will be stealing medication to give to loved ones and giving their patients sugar pills. If it's just one city or region affected, deliveries and transport to that area may slow to a trickle. Even assuming distribution of appropriate medication to emergency workers, it will be difficult to deploy enough police officers to maintain order. Fires may burn out of control because firefighters are sick and transport systems and hospitals may not be fully staffed. All this speaks to the need for better planning and more self–sufficiency.

In the province of Ontario, where I live, "An Act to Provide Formulation and Implementation of Emergency Plans (The Emergency Plans Act)" allows municipalities to pass bylaws dealing with the provision of services during a disaster. Municipalities' plans written under this act deal with financial matters, emergency powers, the duties of municipal council members, training, the distribution of supplies, evacuation and other matters. Council may declare an emergency and take appropriate action. In many plans, there is reference to social service agencies helping to care for and evacuate residents with special needs.

I have worked with some of these agencies who tell me that while they may be handed these responsibilities, they have no budget, no equipment and no training to fulfil them. They have a capability on paper – but real crises happen in real time, on our streets – not on paper. So, how will an emergency unfold in a given community? The best answer lies in research that has been done into past emer-gencies. However, after reviewing many academic studies and reading a lot of emergency plans I have to conclude the signs are not encouraging.

Almost certainly there will be confusion and contradiction. Hurricane Katrina prompted the largest military deployment on US soil since the Civil War, but the emergency response in, and evacuation of, New Orleans encountered huge problems. Ironically, the money and attention showered on response organizations, especially the Department of Homeland Security, after 9/11 probably made things worse because they focused attention on terrorism, not natural disasters.

One of the biggest problems was that New Orleans didn't have enough buses to handle a mass evacuation – even though it knew that 60 per cent of its citizens had no access to transport, either private or public. The oversight is remarkable because buses have many uses. They can not only evacuate people in an emergency but also carry relief workers and supplies in and out of affected areas. They can also provide temporary shelter.

I learned from Al Zaharko, a businessman who has operated several urban bus lines in British Columbia, that buses are an important part of emergency response plans in that province. They attend at fires and other events according to an agreement with the provincial government and compensation follows. Such a system would have helped in New Orleans. Perhaps it should also be adopted by other large cities, with large numbers of people who don't rely on cars for their local transportation needs.

In America's largest 20 cities, between one quarter and one half of residents don't own cars.

Researchers have concluded that many emergency plans are little more than 'fantasy' that rest on false hopes that private transport will be adequate, buses will be available, stadiums will be available to accommodate large numbers of refugees and fuel will be adequate for emergency and private vehicles.

One estimate is that it could take 50 hours to evacuate one million people by car in a typical city setting. Two–car families take both cars, tow trailers, load up mobile homes

*Hurricane Sandy brought flooded avenues in Manhattan's East Village in 2012. Much of what is now downtown in many of our cities was once underwater. Many cities have regular floods and we need urban vegetation and design which can reduce the impact.*

and drive over–cautiously or erratically. The causes of many emergencies – storms, toxic fumes, fires and so on – might thus be moving more quickly than long lines of vehicles on crowded escape routes.

We should also remember that there were more deaths as a result of the evacuation during Hurricane Rita in Houston than were caused directly by the hurricane itself. So the act of evacuation presents a range of risks that may be greater than the reason for calling for an evacuation.

Interestingly, there is scant reference to evacuation in Toronto's emergency plan, even though we know from what happened in New Orleans and Houston in 2005 that evacuations from disaster zones can create their own crises if not planned and rehearsed. Two short paragraphs deal with the need for a decision–making process and the need for "a description of responsibilities to conduct the evacuation, and the process for re–entry." There is reference to the fact that "emergencies are diverse in nature" and to the difficulty in creating a "plan that has a detailed account of the duties involved." There may be more information in other documents, but good crisis response should not involve a trip to the library or a major research project to find documents which may be of help.

It seems obvious that explaining the need for a task is not the same as listing ways and means to accomplish that task. Pointing out how difficult a task may be is not a significant step toward getting the task done. Nor is directing the reader to track down other documents that may or may not be relevant. This public document gives citizens little direction on what to do or not to do in a crisis.

But a real–life adventure may point to how determined people can make a real difference without waiting for instructions. During Hurricane Katrina, three university students drove to New Orleans to see if they could help. They impersonated reporters to get through National Guard checkpoints and were soon at the Superdome, which was being used as an emergency shelter. They made two trips in and out with evacuees, according to a report published by MTV. The irony is that if students could do this in an ordinary car, why couldn't the police, National Guard or other official responders whose mission it was to rescue citizens?

# Defining Evacuation

It may seem obvious that the term 'evacuation' defines itself and needs little discussion. However, consider the evacuation that takes too long, injures evacuees or leaves too many special needs people behind. Consider the possibility of a place being overwhelmed when people resettle there. In reality evacuation can amount to merely relocating a problem. Is an evacuation that does more harm than good worth speaking about and planning for? We need a more precise definition. Here's one from an academic study by two professors at the New Jersey Institute of Technology, Stephen Chien and Vivek Korikanthimath:

*"Efficient evacuation can be defined as a process to safely transport people and goods away from a place or an area within an acceptable time period in an orderly fashion."*

The type of event can dictate an even more precise definition of evacuation. In an emergency that comes upon a city instantly, there may be a need for 'simultaneous' evacuation. If there is some advance warning notice of the event, then evacuation may take places in stages. As the same study indicates:

*"Under simultaneous evacuation, all vehicles are evacuated concurrently; on the other hand, in staging, vehicles are evacuated by zones in a particular sequence."*

The increased degree of difficulty in simultaneous evacuation with no notice is obvious – too many people and vehicles trying to use the same routes at the same time. Of course police could be used to help smooth out the process, but this presumes enough order and infrastructure remain to deploy police, and enough healthy police officers to perform tasks at hand.

Also, evacuating one community may cause problems for others – but the people in danger or facing hardship have to go somewhere. So, perhaps the real question is how to move large numbers of people around, rather than just relocating them.

In some emergencies it may be better to have them stay put and be safe where they are. It's not difficult to imagine weather–related or other events such as gas leaks or even terror attacks that make it risky or impossible to move freely outdoors in a city. Roads may be impassable because of snow, ice, fire, snipers, or sarin gas. But, staying indoors might be the best option anyway. As it happens, staying

**The Hancock Center, Chicago**
*Large, mixed–use buildings have held promise for intensification in urban areas. But they present challenges when needed for shelter or when evacuation is ordered.*

indoors, shutting the windows and turning off the air circulation are normal directions during a chemical release, for example. Similarly, a lack of food, potable water, electricity, or the threat of terrorism might make evacuation the best option. In a pandemic, both options may be invoked. In a large city we could find one neighbourhood evacuated, another in which residents are told to stay in their homes and a third congested by an influx of new arrivals. Furthermore the status of neighbourhoods could change without warning.

Ironically, both staying put and evacuation may be the methods used in the same event at the same time. It's easy to imagine police check–points requiring citizens to prove they have a cottage or relative to stay with in order to use a certain highway or leave a neighbourhood. Restricting mobility might go hand in hand with requiring those same people to fend for themselves on the road a few hours later. But the best strategy could also be to keep all those people off the roads and in their offices, apartments, condos and homes – so–called 'sheltering in place.'

We also need to consider those who can, but won't evacuate. During Hurricane Ike in Galveston in 2008, an evacuation notice warned those who stayed that they faced certain death. Yet about 30 percent of people in the mandatory evacuation zone chose to ignore the order. More than 74 people died and another 3,500 had to be rescued. All communities include groups of people with special needs, like the elderly, who find it hard to leave even if they want to. Often, older people living alone won't leave their homes without their pets. For many years now I've been advising emergency responders to have a ready supply of pet cages if they want seniors to evacuate their homes!

Other studies have shown that even able–bodied residents who wish to heed evacuation orders are at risk.

In an evacuation, traffic will be as slow or more likely, much slower than in normal times. As traffic slows, cars will run out of fuel and make congestion worse. Some drivers may turn off air conditioning, making heat worse and their need for scarce water greater. There will be few facilities on evacuation routes.

If these warnings are late, residents can be trapped by fires or other hazards. This led Australia to adopt a model known as "Prepare, Stay and Defend or Go Early," in the belief that threats from fast–moving brush fires and the like can be lessened by building fire–resistant homes and using fire resistant landscaping. But after 'Black Saturday' in 2009, when more than 170 people were killed by fast–moving brush fires in Victoria State, that policy has been brought into question both in Australia and elsewhere. Parts of California, including Orange County, once considered adopting the Australian approach but later abandoned it.

Whether the approach is stay put or evacuation, effective transport systems will save lives. If it's stay put, there would still be the need to move food, medical supplies and responders around an affected area. If 30% of truckers, transit drivers, taxi drivers and all others in the workforce were dead, sick or pretending to be sick, we would need some way to continue to move citizens, supplies and emergency workers around. Since overcrowding in transport systems spreads disease, redundant systems which lighten the load will help. Toronto's experience with the outbreak of SARS showed that some hospital workers could have spread the disease by wearing scrubs outside hospitals, including on public transit. It also showed that we can't easily quarantine emergency workers.

Regardless of why or whether we stay put or move, one of the major principles in crisis planning is to respond to and plan for effects, not causes. The central issue is our ability to evacuate our city and move our citizens around, rather than why we might want to do so. A viable solution can be a solution to multiple problems. Multiple problems can trigger the same solution, well captured in the notion of isomorphic learning or actioned learning, handed down from systems theory. The ability to move citizens and medical supplies around quickly is also a reason for an efficient urban transport and health system – which we all want anyway.

There is a parallel between a city's fitness and our personal fitness. First, health and fitness are often not a big focus for young people. They are important issues, but not urgent. In a rapidly expanding city, matters other than health and fitness may be a focus. It's only when the city begins to grow and prosper that we turn our attention to quality of life issues. Cities and individuals can neglect personal fitness for a time (in our 20s and even 30s for example) without too many problems. But if we continue to neglect health and fitness, these issues move from being important to being urgent and much harder to deal with. It's best to keep addressing the issue of personal and urban fitness as if it were urgent right now, because it just might be.

Those of us who exercise regularly do so for different reasons. For some, it's the socializing in gyms that's the attraction. It's a way to get out of the house or office for a bit, a break in the middle of the day, weekend recreation, business networking or the possibility of meeting a mate. All are legitimate motivators. For me, it's risk management.

I am becoming fit and trying to stay fit for an unknown specific challenge in the future. By exercising today, have I prevented a heart attack on that occasion off in the future when I have to run to catch a bus? Have I just created the capability of catching that bus and thus not ruining my vacation or missing a meeting? Have I lowered blood pressure or cholesterol and prevented health issues in that way? Perhaps I have. But have I also put a spring in my step and prolonged my life in the workforce? I am certainly more comfortable in my daily activities and I might even look better.

How we quantify and justify fitness is an open question for us all to consider. How cities justify and define a safer environment is equally open. There may be few people who focus on the catastrophic implications of being unfit as a person or as a city. But that doesn't mean that surrogate issues can't be a valid focus. In the case of personal fitness, this may be networking or meeting a mate as described above. In the case of cities, the various manifestations of fitness can be thought of in terms of tourism, air quality, traffic, and landscaping. There can be several end results on both the personal and the urban level.

One reason to work towards safety at the municipal level is that there is a vacuum in the chain of command in crisis and disaster management. I imagine a truck load of toys or appliances taking up valuable space on our major highways during a crisis. There doesn't appear to be anyone with the authority to take that rig off the road, dump the cargo and force the driver to load up with food or medical supplies, and direct the truck to where it's needed. Until we have new emergency plans and a new legal and administrative regime, we need our civic leaders to take action to keep our cities safe.

Another reason to work at the local level to keep cities safer is the lessons learned from others. A general dictum of crisis management is that individuals usually perform well and organizations perform poorly. Inasmuch as we have a coherent intergovernmental response plan (I would argue we don't), the bureaucracy will probably not function well in a crisis. After Hurricane Katrina, a study by researchers John Kiefer and Robert Montjoy at the University of New Orleans found:

> *"...only one thing disintegrated as fast as the earthen levees that were supposed to protect the city [New Orleans], and that was the intergovernmental relationship that is supposed to connect local, state and federal officials before, during and after such a catastrophe."*

# 6

# Evacuation: The Reality

I suspect most of us think that evacuation would consist of getting in our cars and driving out of our city. We might put a few more people into the car, but basically it would be just like a long weekend traffic jam, but more so. I don't think many people can imagine the trouble that might occur. First, I don't think anyone would be prepared for the slowness of the traffic.

Most residents of the cities in North America probably have a dim view of their local traffic congestion. However I've driven up and down New York City's West Side Highway, Cross Bronx Expressway and Long Island Parkway at all times of the day and all seasons of the year. I've also driven the freeways of Los Angeles. These roads are a dream compared to the highways that move traffic in and around my city of Toronto: The Don Valley Parkway, the Gardiner Expressway, the Queen Elizabeth Way and Highways 400, 401 and 427. Driving on these roads is more a like nightmare – at any time of the day – with cars and trucks lucky to be moving at 30 kph (18 mph). In my opinion, if we can figure out an efficient evacuation system for Toronto then any city can!

Studies of evacuations triggered by hurricanes have documented massive jams of slow–moving traffic as evacuees follow advice or orders to 'get out of town.' For people who have special dietary needs, who are on medication, who need to use washrooms or who must eat

*Opposite: Most gridlock is remarkably orderly. Imagine what the scene opposite would be like if a few cars were out of gas, having mechanical problems and fights were breaking out? Studies show that evacuees try to bring all their vehicles with them, tow trailers and load their vehicles down with possessions. 'Contra flow' turns inbound lanes into outbound evacuation lanes. This may increase traffic volume by 70%, at best. But, while moving more people out of a city, contra flow will impede the inflow of emergency responders and supplies.*

regularly, this kind of experience would be a crisis in itself. In many cases the long traffic delays caused cars and trucks to run out of fuel, further clogging the roads. Gas stations sold out and had no hope of being refuelled because of the clogged streets and highways. Power outages made gas stations useless even if they had fuel.

If we had advance warning of a possible evacuation we could ask citizens to keep the tanks in their cars and trucks topped up with fuel. We might also park tanker trucks in strategic locations along evacuation routes and in parks, parking lots, schoolyards and other areas as emergency fuelling stations. But we will have mixed and unpredictable results. Even without aggressive drivers using the shoulders of the roads, there would be little hope of moving a gasoline tanker truck along our limited access highways. In the oil embargoes of the 1970s there was violence in the line ups to buy gasoline in some of America's big cities. There was no reason for concern then other than a lack of gas. But in today's world, if you add terrorism, a pandemic or other frightening occurrence to the mix, surely violence is almost a certainty. It's easy to imagine helpful citizens pushing stalled cars to the side of the road and right over the edge into a ravine. It's easy to imagine fights, possibly including weapons.

So failing to plan and relying on existing infrastructure is not an adequate plan. Louisiana has had experience with this, and with relying on individuals to take action. That state's Emergency Operations plan reads:

*"The primary means of hurricane evacuation will be personal vehicles. School and municipal buses, government–owned vehicles and vehicles provided by volunteer agencies may be used to provide transportation for individuals who lack transportation and require assistance in evacuating."*

As we saw after Hurricane Katrina, and as I see in the many plans I read every year, stating on paper that something will happen is no guarantee that it will.

Some jurisdictions have tried to make better use of existing infrastructure by relying on something called 'contra flow.' This is an emergency plan that allows traffic on all lanes of certain highways to flow in the same direction – away from danger. As with many plans the wonder is that it had to be discovered. During Hurricane Georges in 1998 people trying to leave New Orleans for Baton Rouge on Interstate 10 found themselves stalled in traffic–choked lanes, while the lanes heading back into the city were completely empty. The first test of a contra flow plan was in 2004, during Hurricane Ivan. It was a failure. Traffic flow was anything but smooth: For some the normal two hour journey from New Orleans to Baton Rouge took an exhausting fourteen hours. This isn't surprising when you think of the problems of suddenly converting exit ramps into access ramps and altering the necessary road signs.

Contra flow worked better after governments spent $7.5 million in new ramps and signage for that highway. Unfortunately contra flow didn't serve New Orleans well in Hurricane Katrina either.

Brian Wolshon, a transport specialist at Louisiana State University, has described contra flow as "potentially life threatening." On reason he gives is that impact attenuators and guard rails are not designed to help north bound traffic on a south bound road (or east–west) and vice versa. Even if contra flow doesn't take lives, the gain in volume of traffic by designating all lanes one way is not double normal capacity, but perhaps 70% more. Large numbers of police officers are needed to ensure ramps are used in the new and safe way. Full contra flow can prevent the movement of emergency supplies and responders into the affected area that is being evacuated. In short, Wolshon says the drawbacks almost outweigh the advantages.

There are those who engage in wishful thinking by assuming that car–pooling can be mandated during an evacuation, and this will reduce the volume of traffic. This is a worthy goal, but practically impossible. Police would be in the preposterous position of encouraging strangers to use the same car, creating possible danger and liability. They would also be in the position of preventing single–occupant vehicles from using the road, causing those drivers to park in available locations where their cars and belongings would be vulnerable. Those abandoned cars might also block the movement of other cars or emergency vehicles. Moreover, those drivers would have to fend for themselves, creating more potential danger. Some measures which involve a significant behavioural change such as car–pooling are best promoted in normal times so that the approach is used in emergencies with less resistance and liability.

The harsh reality is that in an emergency evacuation of any large urban area, there will never be enough routes available with the capacity to handle the flow smoothly. Plus, the cost of adapting and upgrading existing infrastructure may be prohibitive.

So what can we do? It's doubtful that a public communication campaign could change behaviour to cause average citizens to keep their cars tuned up, full of gas and packed with emergency food, water, clothing and such. This is just the kind of behavioural change that I suspect could be implemented in Japan, but not in Canada or the US. In fact, in Japan, where I've conducted several emergency exercises including an earthquake simulation, most citizens sleep with shoes under their beds so they can protect their feet from the shards of glass that will cover the floor in the event of a quake. They have backpacks nearby with food, water and clothing in them. Most Japanese keep a little bag of sand near their gas stoves in case they need to smother an open flame.

On the margins, some North American citizens might see the merits in these small changes, but I suspect that most people will not change behaviour, even if there is an obvious advantage to be had. Most drivers are aware that if they keep their cars tuned, tires inflated, drive more slowly and so on, they will save money. Few take any notice.

In North America we have become used to relying on affordable energy to make our lives easier and more comfortable. We tend to overheat our homes and offices in winter and make them too cold in summer. Haven't we all come across office workers who secretly run space heaters under their desks in the summer to counter the effects of air conditioning?

If people cannot be convinced to take actions that would be in their best self interests, then this is something that emergency plans have to take into account. Indeed, the human condition may be even more complex than the contradiction between behaviour and obvious self–interest would indicate. Perhaps the workers with the space heaters are rebelling against a monolithic employer or the multinational owners of a 60 story office tower. Perhaps drivers are rebelling against multinational oil companies and exhibiting their own freedom, even to act in a way detrimental to their own interests. People reserve the right to engage in activities, even those which are harmful to them. These are large issues which won't be fully addressed here but we must be aware of them during public communication campaigns.

I can point to two instances in which large scale behaviour patterns have been changed for the better. The first involves the trend to fitness, especially jogging, in the 1970s. It appeared that this change took place overnight. One day the norm seemed to involve smoking, drinking and sedentary behaviour. The next day it appeared to be jogging togs, followed by exercise class and private gyms. It is said that pollster George Gallop was fascinated with this inexplicable change in core values which usually takes decades to materialize. Perhaps the explanation lies in the multiple motivations to change. Fitness became a core value for the good feeling it generated, longevity, and the socializing in running groups and fitness clubs.

The second change in behaviour in my lifetime involved drinking and driving. Drinking and driving, as depicted in movies and joked about among people a little older than I, was considered 'boys' night out.' Smashing up cars, barely making it home and laughing about it was not unusual. Drinking and driving quickly became unacceptable behaviour, especially in urban areas, and social pressure appears to have been at least as powerful as the force of laws.

These two issues may have something in common. Perhaps in both there are multiple pressures on the people whose behaviour changed. There was some personal reward (health and safety). There was external pressure (peer and law). And there may have been a social reward – socializing in fitness settings and being able to socialize more safely without the combination of alcohol and driving.

Nonetheless, the overriding lesson may be that public policy needs multiple justifications. Public policy may also need multiple rewards in order to be supported. In case this is an incorrect assumption, there is still no harm in advocating a public policy measure for several reasons and pointing out the several benefits to the citizenry who adopt the measure. If one hoped–for benefit doesn't come to pass, the others may be ample justification for the policy.

However, before we consider the intricacies of policy making let's look at some easier ways of evacuating urban areas.

# 7

# Mobility

Getting around is so vital to most of us that it plays a large part in where we choose to live and work – if we happen to be among that small portion of the world's population lucky enough to have a choice. However, we never really think of how we might make maximum use of our mobility to help us reach safety in a large scale emergency or crisis.

Like most cities of its size Toronto has a mix of surface and underground transit routes, some dependent on electricity, others on the internal combustion engine. It also has a small ferry system used mainly to get city dwellers to the parks, beaches and sailing clubs located on the islands that form the outer limits of the city's harbour on the north shore of Lake Ontario.

At one time the Toronto Transit Commission (TTC) looked into establishing a commuter ferry system running along the lake shore connecting the western and eastern boundaries of the city. But it abandoned the project after concluding that such a system could be incapacitated by bad weather. This is probably true, but it is also true of our streetcars, trains, buses and expressways. Even if a commuter ferry system were incapacitated three times as often as other systems, this would still only amount to single digit down–days per year. This is hardly a valid a reason to reject it. Ferries are in use all over the world crossing rivers, lakes, harbours, inlets, and even open seas. They vary in size, speed, capacity, reliability and safety. But on any given day millions of people travel by ferry.

Maybe the TTC will change its mind one day. Until then, we'll have to rely on the transit system we have. On the whole it is reasonably efficient and outside peak hours is comfortable.

## Subways

The biggest drawback of Toronto's subway system is that it isn't extensive enough. One U-shaped line runs from the northern suburbs south to the downtown area and up to the northwestern suburbs. Another line runs west to east (across the Don Valley ravine) and connects to the Scarborough Light Rapid Transit, an automated surface rail line. There is also a short spur line running east off the north–south subway, the Sheppard extension. There's no shortage of plans and ideas to build more routes but cost and local political rivalries have proved to be insurmountable obstacles.

It is obvious to users that the subway system is at capacity during rush hours. Cars are packed. Some commuters have to let several trains go by before they can find one with space to board. Some platforms in the downtown area can get dangerously overcrowded during busy times. Even if the system were not crippled by a power shortage or other failure it's safe to assume that it would be unable to cope with the stress of a mass evacuation. Perhaps even worse, a breakdown in the system while packed trains were between stations would only add to the crisis.

## Trains

We are fortunate to have commuter trains with double decker cars for extra capacity. They are diesel powered so they would not grind to a halt if there were a loss of electric power. Coordination is another matter. Our transcontinental passenger trains are slowed down by level crossings. They must compete with freight trains for the same tracks, and freight is given priority. Within the city, we have too few commuter stops on our heavy rail lines.

## Streetcars

Toronto's streetcars (or trams) appear to offer a way out, if necessary. They operate on east–west and north–south routes and are ubiquitous, at least in the downtown. But these vehicles have limitations. Their average speed is slow. The capacity of individual cars and articulated cars is acceptable, but the ability to move people across distances over time is the ultimate determinant of a transport system in good times and bad. This system is not adequate.

There are other factors that would impair their value in an emergency. One that is relevant for evacuation scenarios is manoeuvrability. During emergencies there will be disabled vehicles, cars and trucks going the wrong way, emergency vehicles going in every direction, crowds, and other obstacles impeding the movement of surface traffic. Because they use rails, streetcars can only stop or go. They have no capability to move left or right in traffic, and metal wheels on metal rails increase starting and stopping times. Metal wheels on metal rails also mean more danger for pedestrians if they're involved in an accident with a streetcar. Metal severs bodies. Rubber tires crush, but more pedestrians survive.

A close relative of the streetcar is the rubber–tired trolley bus. It too is dependent on overhead wires for its electric power but it is much more manoeuvrable than a streetcar. Unfortunately, Toronto scrapped its trolley fleet some years ago and replaced them with less manoeuvrable streetcars.

## Buses

Buses are more manoeuvrable and versatile than subways, trains or streetcars. They can change their routes at will, refuel and take a different route after unloading passengers. There may be emergencies in which these buses need to be pressed into service to take full loads of passengers out of the city after abandoning their normal routes.

So, more buses could be part of the answer if we are looking for ways to move large numbers of people out of

harm's way. It's hard to see taxpayers or their local governments approving the purchase of extra buses just in case they might be needed in an emergency. However, the conversion of some streetcar routes to bus routes probably would be acceptable to the public. The unit costs for buses is less than streetcars and they would be of more use in an emergency. Antique streetcars could be kept on certain routes as tourist attractions, for sightseeing, and for special events.

The most promising use of buses is as surface subways. Long articulated buses on dedicated lanes can compete in capacity and speed with underground subways. Large doors and platforms level with the floor of the buses can mean they empty and fill in seconds.

## Personal (Self–Powered) Transport

Self–powered transport of a variety of types is thought to be of great use in an evacuation. A common statistic is that a reasonably fit person can walk about four miles per hour. Thus in a long day, with rest stops, that person should be able to cover up to 40 miles. In most cases that would take a person well outside a danger zone. People using bicycles – or even roller blades – might be able to cover longer distances.

But there would still be problems.

I'm reasonably fit and if time permits I will walk for an hour to a business meeting or event and then walk back

*Corktown Common, Toronto*
*In an evacuation, even the fittest residents will need regular rest stations and water fountains. We can improve our path and park networks for regular use and make a more liveable city. If these facilities are needed in an emergency, they may save lives. If not, their existence is a payoff in itself.*

I've enjoyed biking and rollerblading around much of Toronto but neither mode co–exists well with other forms of traffic on crowded urban streets – and even less with pedestrians on crowded sidewalks. In an evacuation, the friction would be so much worse. My conclusion is that we can't rely on personal, self–powered transport in an emergency. We can only encourage its use by those who can handle it. We can also make our city friendly and safe for all types of transport.

We can start by acting on the truism that people will never take a walking route they don't know exists. Thus, the first step is to use signage to tell people where ravines, trails, parks and attractions are, how far away they are, and the approximate walking time to them. This policy would have several obvious benefits in normal times. It would encourage more urban walking and thus a fitter population. It might even reduce peak–hour stresses on the transit system.

Signage can provide additional information for those with special needs. People using mobility scooters may want to know the type of surface they will be on – wood chips, gravel, pavement, grass and so on. Some blind people prefer gravel which alerts them to whether there are other users on the trail. Rollerbladers need hard surfaces. More information can help more people use these special modes of transport.

Increased use of the paths, trails and routes through the city's parks and ravines will require some investment

to my office or hotel. On most days in London, Paris, New York and other cities, I walk for at least an hour. But I had a reality check in Vancouver recently. I was laying over for a day on my way to an assignment and decided to walk around Stanley Park, one of the largest urban parks in North America. The trip around the remarkable setting was a little over two hours. But this was non–stop walking without rest – not an hour with a rest while I conducted my business – and then another walk.

Halfway through I learned I was wearing the wrong shoes for a long trek and had trouble finishing. This made me realize that most people, in the wrong shoes, or without good socks, or who are not used to long walks, couldn't really cover the distance that statistics indicate they might.

in extra infrastructure such as drinking–water fountains, shelters, benches, toilets and other amenities. These are all normal park, ravine and pathway amenities found in the existing park systems in most cities and are unlikely to spark either controversy over cost, or alarm over their value in an emergency. Many improvements would be seen as normal maintenance and appropriate expansion of park systems. Much could be achieved within existing budgets. More could be achieved by using development fees, site plan controls and other methods of negotiating concessions with developers of condominiums and office buildings. It would also be advisable to engage in public consultations with residents about the amenities they might want to see in their parks, ravines and trails.

As we've seen, people relying on their own power can only travel so far. So the next step should involve the examination of what might be termed 'concentric circles of mobility.' If planners estimated how far a special needs person can travel in one day, there could be shelters and signage at that location to assist those who make it that far. The signage could indicate if there are private amenities nearby such as restaurants and shelter. Other circles could estimate the distance fit people can walk, cyclists can cycle, rollerbladers can travel and so on. Each circle would

An informative map for visitors wishing to explore a canyon in Alberta. Few people will seek out a destination they don't know exists. Distance markers and route signs can encourage walking and inform tourists about attractions.

effectively form a staging ground for the next day's travels, or perhaps the return home.

The end of subway and streetcar lines will also become staging grounds. At some, there may be transit buses ready to take some residents on another leg of their journeys – but to where? Assuming a major evacuation, there will be a shortage of fuel in gas stations. If this is the case, another de facto staging ground will be the spot at which city buses run out of fuel. We must plot this location and plan accordingly.

# Redundancy

I became convinced of the importance of building extra, or redundant, capacity into emergency plans many years ago when I was touring an oil refinery. I asked about the implications if a large storage tank ruptured and spilled huge amounts of gasoline, diesel or other potentially dangerous liquids. My guide explained that earthen berms surrounded each tank and would contain the spill. Furthermore, there was a policy to construct the berms so that they could contain 110% of the capacity of the tank. There was redundant capacity – and the concept stayed with me.

A transit system can become useless in many ways. It could be severe weather or a (rare) act of terror that may make the system inoperable. Much more common are technical failures, accidents, union–management friction, and (particularly in subways) suicide attempts. A single stalled streetcar or tram can effectively disable all traffic behind it, including other streetcars, buses, trucks and cars. An evacuation notice can quickly overwhelm a transit system as well as streets and highways. For this reason, it's sound public policy to create a redundant capacity in our transport systems.

But what does redundancy mean? Our cities could define redundancy as the capacity to move 110% the population at any given time. That would be a tall order. Or it could be defined as the capacity to move 110% of the people who need to be transported (perhaps the actual population minus those who will stay put in homes, hospitals and businesses). Redundancy could mean multiple systems (subways, buses, streetcars, monorails, etc.) heading in the same general direction, or the number of optional routes evacuees have at their disposal.

However, it is clear that in an emergency we would also need to keep as many private vehicles off the road as

*Opposite: Traffic gridlock is a regular feature of our urban roads. Crisis planners who think that evacuations by car will go smoothly are engaged in wishful thinking. The articulated bus pictured here carries more people, but is not very maneuverable. Disabled rubber–tired buses can be pushed out of the way if they are disabled, but very large buses and steel wheeled streetcars which become disabled will be dead weight in the street and make emergencies much worse.*

possible to reduce congestion. But we can't hope to do that unless we can offer alternative transport systems, and these could be defined as redundant, or perhaps in excess of immediate, daily needs.

Some cities have specified evacuation routes which are marked for easy identification. But this is counter to the flexibility that motorists show during normal times. Drivers choose routes intuitively, based on traffic reports or because of signage on their route, or even to create some variety in their daily commutes. In theory it shouldn't concern us how drivers chose to exit an evacuation zone if they can do so safely and without hindering others. In practice this will depend on the area having enough routes and options so that evacuees are not penalized for their creative and flexible choices.

We are surrounded by examples of redundancy in our daily lives. A butcher shop doesn't use a scale that will only handle one pound to weigh cuts of meat weighing one pound. The scale has a capacity beyond the weight of what will be weighed to accommodate the additional force at the moment of impact. The same is true of hoists in garages, bridges, and so on. It would be logical to have planning measures in place to create a capacity in the transport system in excess of the normal and usual number of people it serves.

Redundancy in transport systems will also serve us well in non-crisis times, but attaining that goal will not be easy. The densest population in Canada is in 'The Golden Horseshoe' around the northwest end of Lake Ontario. It takes in the Greater Toronto Area and stretches southwest to take in the City of Hamilton. In just fifteen years (1986–2001) the population here increased by 30 per cent and is expected to increase by another 30 per cent by 2031. Study after study has shown the need for much greater investment in public transportation. They also indicate there is little possibility of widening existing traffic arteries for cars and trucks. There is, however, a $100 billion inter-governmental plan that won't actually take any cars off the roads: It will just maintain the status quo – for a while.

There are lessons here for all cities. Population growth, increased life expectancy, immigration and higher populations densities are the new normal in industrialized and developed cities. People are migrating to cities in unprecedented numbers. People who live in cities live longer and are healthier. Cities have traditionally lost their ageing population as retirees on fixed incomes seek more cost-effective surroundings in satellite communities. However, there is now a trend to staying in the city in smaller housing units, including condos, to be near services and family. Immigration has always been the key to stable real estate values and a renewed workforce in cities, and this trend is growing. The vast majority of Canadians who move, do so from smaller to larger communities. The vast majority of immigrants to our country settle in our major cities. Increasing density is considered a way to reduce our environmental footprints and make the best use of existing infrastructure. It appears these trends will continue and this will require better emergency planning.

With this background, it's fascinating to think how a city such as Toronto might make progress in its crisis planning, especially evacuation and quarantine, or sheltering in place. The progression I hope for is from gridlock and competition among transit and other agencies to a safer city with redundant transport systems and other public policy initiatives resulting in more time for business and leisure, less pollution, more tourism, the ability to evacuate and other benefits.

One way to look at this transition is through the Utopian planning lens. The memo at the end of this book, reporting on the state of a representative neighbourhood on the occasion of the 600th anniversary of European settlement here, is a version of Utopian planning. One tradition in Utopian planning is to think beyond the life spans of existing politicians, residents and planners. This can depoliticize issues and allow us to examine them without the biases we all have because of our current circumstances.

Another way is through what some scholars call 'stage theory.' Stage theory asks, 'How do we get from A to B?' We're all familiar with the child in the back seat of a car who wants to know 'Are we there yet?' The answer is 'No' – but by using traditional stages in the public policy process to explore where the path might lie, I'm hoping

we can speed up the journey. The traditional stages of public policy implementation are:

- Issue Identification
- Issue Analysis
- Citizen Engagement
- Option Development
- Option Evaluation
- Implementation
- Evaluation

This process is often shortened and many in the public policy process skip steps. Proper emergency response skips steps and rushes to action as well. But these traditional stages allow for a full discussion of how difficult it will be to get the issue of safer cities on the public policy agenda. After all, evacuation and emergency planning are not issues that will capture the imagination of politicians or public administrators. The discussion will also point to ways of building a safer city using existing structures and learning from others.

Toronto's SkyDome has been praised for accessibility and washroom facilities. It's wishful thinking though to assume that 70,000 people can take shelter and find enough food and services in such a facility during an emergency. A by–law could require such facilities to keep enough on hand for a week for a maximum crowd.

# Seven Stages of Planning

## 1. Issue Identification

Where do new initiatives in public policy come from? There is a formal process through which the non–partisan civil service manages and brings forward issues for consideration by the government of the day. There is also a formal process by which political staff prepare for Question Period in provincial legislatures and in the House of Commons. Most city governments lack an organized opposition or formal political parties, but do have both a civil service staff and political aids to manage agendas in formal ways. Parliamentary committees and the Senate (upper chamber) occasionally play important roles in the Westminster system. Committees in both chambers are much stronger in the US system, as are non–governmental think–tanks and lobby groups. In the US, you won't find a non–partisan civil service until you get two or three levels below cabinet members.

But there are also other methods by which issues come up for consideration, such as media reports. Question Period in the parliamentary system has been described (jokingly) as the occasion for opposition politicians to read clippings from the national newspapers to the government each day. Also, initiatives from other jurisdictions occasionally seem appealing. Often it's a politician trying to emulate another successful politician, or a civil servant trying to adopt an initiative from another jurisdiction he admires.

In Toronto, Paul Godfrey, former Chair of the now abandoned Metropolitan level of government, told me how he became interested in championing a sports stadium for the city. First, he was intrigued to learn that Houston was most support. It may include people who tried to join the evacuation or stay at home, before deciding to find temporary accommodation. Their care will require considerable planning and therefore could be most problematic.

To begin with, cities have many large facilities that are *temporary* homes for thousands of people at a time. These include office buildings, schools, sports stadiums, arenas, places of worship and so on. Most have washrooms and some facilities to feed people. However, as events in New Orleans proved, large arenas are not meant to accommodate people outside the controlled conditions of sports matches or special events. This problem could be addressed by requiring facilities to have emergency generators capable of providing power for several days. Similarly, they could be required to stock enough food and water to satisfy 110% of their capacity for several days.

This is the opposite of just–in–time delivery, common to most businesses. It would require storage space and inventory control, but shouldn't be a burden beyond the initial expenditure because the inventory would turn over every few events.

The policy of keeping additional supplies on hand would have to be negotiated with facility owners and managers. It's easy to imagine resistance to change and even a public communication campaign fighting the initiative by raising the price of tickets to cause patrons to pay for the supplies. It may be that during negotiations, governments would have to offer to underwrite the initial surge in inventory. But I've talked with some large stadium managers who have mutual aid agreements in place with nearby hospitals and who welcome the role of storing redundant supplies.

On a smaller scale, I remember trying to make this case with the operators of a chain of retirement homes. They wanted a crisis plan. It seemed obvious that many facilities in suburban locations could put in gas or wood–burning heating systems to augment oil and electricity. They could insulate to save energy and use generators to both heat and cool. I also advocated uncovering or digging wells on their suburban property to use during emergencies. Their menus could be modified to use stockpiles of food that required less preparation, fewer people, and less water and electricity. Astonishingly, the operator claimed to have these menus in place and was just waiting for government funding to buy the storehouse of supplies needed. I was taken aback at what I thought was abdication and lack of entrepreneurship. I indicated that the only expenditure would be the cost of buying the supplies once. I felt that the cost of this exercise could be easily recouped many times over as a selling point to new clients. Prospective families could be told that they were guaranteed a two–week supply of food, water and power in the event of any shortage. Why wait for the government to take an initiative that is within your core mandate?

There is another motivating factor for sports stadiums, arenas and possibly many other institutions. Evacuees and people in need will flood these institutions regardless of whether these facilities fit within an urban evacuation plan. They will look for shelter somewhere large and safe and then look for food. They went to the Louisiana Superdome during hurricanes even before Katrina and vandalized furnishings, broke into skyboxes, and looted vending machines, according to news reports.

Then hygiene becomes a problem. Toilet facilities in these buildings are designed for several quick trips for a capacity crowd for a few hours. Few are equipped with showers. Here again, facilities could be required to store extra portable toilets or identify outside areas where outhouses could be installed quickly. Portable outside showers for use in good weather or indoors where there is proper drainage would also be required. Several emergency response suppliers sell portable showers which can accommodate dozens of people at a time.

In rapid evacuations people often arrive at temporary shelters in sleepwear and little else. Those who are forbidden

*Sunrise Propane Explosion, Toronto.*
*In 2008, illegal transfer practices led to a massive explosion that caused traffic chaos and forced thousands from their homes to seek shelter at York University. What would have happened if this incident had happened during winter in freezing conditions when the dorms would already be full?*

# 4. Option Development

There are several policy options open to a public administrator. These range from non–coercive communication designed to change behaviour and attitudes, through to laws restricting behaviour with penalties for non–compliance. One can't legislate the use of a transport system, but governments (provinces and the national government in Canada) certainly could require municipalities to have redundant systems through legislation or the transfer of funds for this stated purpose. Mayors could interpret current legislation to mean they have both the power and requirement to have emergency plans to evacuate and thus the infrastructure to do so. Once the transport systems and other amenities were in place, public information campaigns could help drive citizens to use the systems. This is so–called 'demand management' which uses information, pricing, convenience and other measures to discourage some activities and encourage others. Legislation may require action by municipalities, but there also needs to be motivation and public communication to ensure success.

Money is often the motivator. It is one of the tools in the demand management toolbox. The high price of goods or services to users may be a deterrent at certain levels. By advocating tolls on some roads we could make some drivers move from their cars to one of several mass transit systems.

Given the public's resistance to change and our history of free roadways, a compromise might be required. Choice would be at the heart of the compromise. If commuters had a choice among several types of transport, they might be willing to accept some toll roads.

In my community, the choices could include: Subway, GO commuter trains, buses, VIA interurban trains, commuter ferry, monorail, and streetcar in a line along the lake, between Oakville and Oshawa. The publicizing of these several choices might cause drivers to accept a limited toll on the parallel Gardiner Expressway, Queen Elizabeth Way and perhaps even other highways such as the 401 and Don Valley Parkway. A limited toll could involve using a transponder system similar to that on the fully–tolled 407 highway to the north of Toronto. Perhaps one lane of these other highways could feature a toll that drivers could voluntarily choose to access at a cost. This one lane could be better maintained with a higher speed limit, thus illustrating the direct benefit for the small fee paid. A further incentive could involve the use of toll zones, license plate restrictions, or parking fees.

In the context of evacuation, option development needs to be the development of component options, and the use of multiple agencies to develop and deliver them. Component options and outcomes include better transport systems, less commute time, iconic urban symbols, tourism, cleaner air and so on. In terms of multiple agencies, it's hard to imagine that any level of government or even all levels of government could fund and implement the kind of infrastructure projects required. All governments would have to be actively involved and the projects would have to access multiple funding sources. The private sector would have to be involved as well, along with community groups, coalitions and individuals.

# 5. Option Evaluation

A simple cost–benefit analysis might show that many projects, far less ambitious than these, in a variety of fields, would not pass muster. In health care, for example, a large percentage of budgets are consumed in the last few months of most people's lives. Does this mean we should seriously consider euthanasia or triage during those months in order to save money? Of course not – because our society has placed a moral and ethical value on keeping people alive with available medicine and techniques that do no harm. If we do need to examine monetary value, we can look at the health care budgets for geriatric medicine and palliative care

Perhaps we should ask what would be the consequences of not using our medical knowledge and equipment to prolong the quality and quantity of life within reason. What kind of a society would we be if we used neglect, triage and unregulated euthanasia to save money? What would be the psychological consequences to all members of society, especially those who must decide when to use neglect, triage and euthanasia? Some of the consequences could be quantified in stress, the effect on the immune system, Post Traumatic Stress Disorder (PTSD), critical incident stress, chronic stress and so on. These ailments would have to be treated – and that would be at a cost. Other consequences might include so–called mission creep. Once a euthanasia program were in place, where would it end? Would it extend to those with genetic disorders, religious affiliation, sexual orientation and might these criteria be used with foetuses in utero? We have precedents both in history and in contemporary practice that should cause a society to be cautions about mission creep of this kind.

So redundant infrastructure to assist with potential mass evacuation probably would not pass a strict cost–benefit analysis. But we then might ask, what kind of city or what kind of society are we building if we can't evacuate our citizens in times of emergency? This is not as dramatic a question as the medical one above, but it is a start. What is also important is to consider how much utility the initiative has, and how much might be wasted in an initiative that really has a hidden justification – i.e. an evacuation that may never happen. But just because the infrastructure is never or rarely used for this extraordinary case doesn't mean that the funding was a total waste. If an initiative recovered 70% of its cost, then the waste is 30% not 100%.

Actuaries put a value on human life and revise this by

jurisdiction regularly. If redundant transport systems take cars off the road there is a great statistical possibility that lives will be saved. One could credit the redundant transport projects with the value of lives saved. Shortfalls in operating expenses could be adjusted commensurately. Time spent in traffic is a loss to the economy and a health hazard because of the stress created. It is relatively easy to track annual changes in the monetary value of reduced commuting time and stress. Similarly, the pollution generated as a result of extra fuel being burned in auto gridlock is quantifiable as are deaths from respiratory ailments. We could also factor in time off work and reduced productivity.

Just because a method of evaluation is difficult, doesn't mean it's impossible. Even if a method of precise evaluation is impossible, this doesn't mean that the project which is defying quantification isn't of value. A current example is the debate over global warming or the competing phrase, climate change. Can't this discussion be circumvented by advocating less pollution? Less pollution has its own rewards, perhaps including less traffic, better health and so on. If less pollution positively affects other issues such as global warming, climate change and even productivity in industry, so much the better. If less pollution also is linked to the development of new technology to combat pollution, this is even better. But if the prime goal of less pollution is the only one we can say with certainty to have been achieved, this is a worthy goal in itself.

# 6. Implementation

"Everything is related to everything else," according to environmentalist Barry Commoner. Options developed are related to the art of the possible. The option that one develops should be one that can be implemented, otherwise why waste efforts in the development stage? While there is value in Utopian planning as an exercise in intellectual stimulation, there is also value in the showing that no new ground is being broken and that the public policy choices have all been made before and proven to work in other jurisdictions. All people involved in the public policy process will have to ponder conditions in their cities to determine if a type of technology or approach to a problem will generate support or opposition. In one community the monorail as a symbol of modernity (albeit Walt Disney's version from 50 years ago) will generate excitement. In others it might be rejected as fanciful.

Any change can be both controversial and politicized. Laws and common sense may insist on public consultations, yet these may well include people who don't wish to be consulted, know or care little about the project, and will have moved away, died or have significantly changed their demographic (age, income, children, etc.) by the time the project comes to fruition. Hence my advocacy for making needed changes in a modular fashion using existing governance structures. This incrementalism may be more palatable to the public.

Time can also depoliticize an issue. Media coverage and musings about how our city will look with new amenities might capture the imagination of those of all political stripes. A plan that imagines the jurisdiction one hundred years from now can capture media and public attention. This is so far in the future that is hard for political antagonists to project their current agendas onto the plan. The Utopian vision at the end of this book features a look at what a Toronto neighbourhood might be like on the 600th anniversary of European arrival in 2092. This is far enough ahead of us – a person's lifetime – that it's hard to push political considerations forward, but it is possible to consider technology and social organization.

There is yet another approach to incrementalism by which we might realize the measures discussed in the report of 2092. Some pilot tests in public policy become permanent. Perhaps the most famous is personal income tax. There seem to be many catalysts to justify a pilot test of new transport systems or the other measures advocated here. For example, Toronto, like most cities, has an annual exhibition. The people who run these fairs are usually known and trusted civic leaders. It would be normal and natural for them to drive a new public policy of having a monorail or gondola through the fair grounds. It would be equally natural to involve the city transit authority to make sure this transport system connects up with existing systems and routes.

Large sports facilities are owned, run or used by successful business people and civic boosters. These organizations are capable of taking on administrative and financial challenges. They could accomplish a task that meets both their legitimate self–interest and the public good. Stadium operators could be reminded that their buildings likely will be staging areas in emergencies, so they might as well prepare. It is also in the best interests of stadiums and arenas to have efficient crowd management. It would seem logical for these corporations to contribute to transport systems that serve their needs during events and also happen to be part of a larger urban transport plan.

**Sky Ride at the Canadian National Exhibtion, Toronto.** *Replacing the popular Alpine Way Gondola that was closed in 1994, this popular chairlift transports people during the exhibition smoothly from one side of the fair to the other. As cable technology becomes part of transit systems worldwide, could a fairground exhibition help to build support for an unfamiliar public transport solution locally?*

*New York Police Department Converted Transit Bus: Offering a large amount of cargo space, this converted transit bus now serves the citizens of New York though a secondary use as a police mobile command center.*

tions might regularly park near high schools for health education purposes, in seniors' neighbourhoods for winter flu vaccinations or near sporting events and concerts just in case of need. Vehicles could also be used as mobile cooling stations in summer heat–waves, warming stations in winter cold spells and to serve the homeless with a range of support services. The police might find a mobile command centre or outreach application for transit vehicles as well.

What are the additional potential uses for our transport systems? Most large cities have art galleries, museums, theatres and concert halls. If each cultural organization sponsored a subway car, streetcar or bus, our cities could have travelling exhibits to promote themselves. The same approach could be used by universities to conduct outreach and even governments to better deliver some services.

In addition to pop–up restaurants and retailers, why not pop–up public services? A streetcar (or other transit vehicle) outfitted as a health station could park in high–need areas and at high–need times of the day. Health sta-

There may be ways to serve disadvantaged populations and neighbourhoods using transit vehicles too. A vehicle outfitted with career counsellors might combat youth unemployment. An emerging neighbourhood experiencing overcrowding would benefit from mobile services (police, fire, EMS, etc.) that were not keeping pace with the needs of the growing population.

And what of the industrial applications for our transit systems? There is already an industrial application that goes relatively unnoticed. Private couriers and the post office use transit systems to transport mail and small packages in large cities. Can this application be expanded? If subways, streetcars, buses, monorails and Skytrains carried purpose built modular containers of mail, perhaps even being sorted while in transit, this application could keep countless postal and courier trucks off the roads and perhaps even close some downtown postal stations. Bulk mail could be delivered to buildings at the end of transit lines and brought into our cities on customized transit vehicles. Letters and packages could then be offloaded to smaller courier and postal vehicles, keeping large trucks off downtown streets.

Farmers' markets, craft sales and flea markets are an enjoyable and useful part of urban life. However, the trucks that bring these goods into the city are not. Farmers and others who have goods to sell could bring their wares to the end of the transit line, rent appropriate square footage in modified transit cars which would then travel to locations all over the city and be parked so the public can shop in or near the vehicles.

What about the unsavoury topic of garbage? Our streets are regularly clogged with large garbage trucks and the frequency of pickup is decreasing. Toronto sends hundreds of trucks per year onto our major highways to landfill sites as far away as Michigan. These trucks present an additional haz-

ard on the roads and cause increased maintenance. Would it be possible to use separate and sealed vehicles or cars to sort and transport garbage to final sorting staging areas at the end of the transit line? Could there be recycling, reusing, burning or other means of disposal at the end of the lines?

There may be other applications for transit systems which would defray costs and facilitate implementation plans. Theoretically, if one car in 20 were being used for a non–transit application, this could represent up to a 5% underwriting of transit costs.

*Our Cities Ourselves – Budapest.*
*One of the long–standing dreams to make cities more liveable is to put more services underground. Mies tried this with garbage disposal. Underground PATH systems and subways move pedestrians and commuters. But what we haven't done is move freight on our underground systems. 150 years ago mail was sorted on railway mail cars and this could be a feature of subways today. Why don't subways haul freight and even garbage in and out of our cities, taking trucks off our roads?*

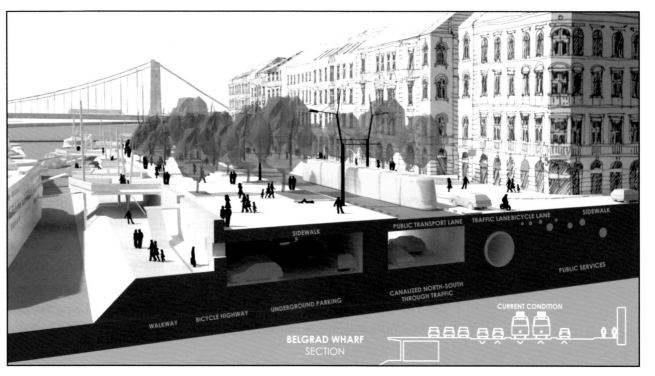

a second or third look that others did not. As a result we categorized some plans as 'inadequate' rather than non–existent, for example. But the effect is much the same. Our search became a metaphor or proxy for the researcher in an NGO, business, school or other institution who is asked to find the city plan and use it as a guide to being better prepared. If the plan can't be found or the jargon not be understood, it's much the same as having no plan or no guidance.

Even a casual comparison reveals a huge variation in definitions and techniques. We might suppose that in all the years after 9/11 and after countless natural disasters there would be some movement towards standardization. Yet such basic elements as job descriptions, organizational charts, and the direction to keep logs are not standardized. Even direction on record–keeping and what portions of plans (if any) should be kept secret is not standard. Variations can be expected for communities as far apart as Brisbane, Australia, San Diego, California, and Calgary, Alberta. The problem arises if emergency services from one community are called in to help a neighbouring community and aren't familiar with the local jargon, definitions and acronyms.

Here's one example. Many of us are familiar with term WMD for weapons of mass destruction. The definition has to be reasonably elastic, but two of the plans in our list define hand grenades as WMD. Many people might think WMD refers to nuclear, biological and chemical weapons.

One can imagine the confusion this might cause to commanders, communicators and responders during an emergency. At the very least responders should know what they have to deal with when they are alerted to the presence of WMD.

It's the same with ICE. You may think 'ICE information' has something to do with winter weather. In some cities' emergency plans it's an acronym for *in case of emergency*. Here are some more:

- "A completed RPA will be transmitted to the FCO for each applicant. If the RPA is denied by the FCO, the POA will notify..." (Jacksonville, Florida)

- "The SCG would act as an interface with DCLG resilience advisers and national government departments. The West Midlands conurbation LRF has an agreed SCG process including activation..." (Birmingham, UK)

- "The local NMDOH representative to EOC will also provide epidemiological and other public health emergency preparedness and response guidance related to the incident the DOH has..." (Albuquerque, New Mexico)

- "The EOC is managed by the MOEM and... WebEOC..." (Baltimore, Maryland)

I recently asked a few young professionals about these terms, just to ensure that I was not the only one unfamiliar with them. I informally canvassed a group of more than a dozen students in a Master's program in urban planning at a leading university. One student knew what ICE information was. The remaining acronyms were just a puzzle. Yet when these students graduate some could be working on co-management agreements between jurisdictions covering response and mutual aid in the event of a large scale emergency.

Only about half the plans reviewed had few, or no, acronyms. The names of the most accessible ten plans for ease of comprehension are listed in the appendix.

Acronyms and jargon are not always bad. They can save time and convey a lot of information. But you have to be sure everyone understands what they mean. An emergency planner would do well to guess that the average citizen would not be familiar with medical, police, security and response jargon. So, when a 20–page city plan has another 1–2 pages of acronyms and special terms, it is excessive. After all, the plan is designed to help residents, businesses and organizations in the city – not just academics and responders with special understanding of emergencies.

Some of the least accessible plans are those in which readers have to wade through several pages of key concepts, methodologies, and descriptions. Twelve in particular (see appendix for "least accessible") spend page after page on their city's history, geography, demography, topography, and other characteristics in addition to offering more pages of lists of terms and definitions.

Pittsburgh, for instance, defines such common words as "activate," "deploy," "direction," "notify," "standby," and "weather watch." Here are some more definitions:

- "Risk is the chance of a hazard occurring multiplied by the impact if that hazard were to occur." (Bradford, UK)

- "Thunderstorms can occur anywhere in the world and at any time of the day..." (Oklahoma City)

- "Self Evacuation: Evacuation from an area under a person's own arrangements." (Brisbane)

- "Although evacuations occur daily in the United States, it is difficult to typify a generic model because evacuations lack both definition and consensus on specific parameters." (Charlotte, North Carolina)

- "An emergency is a situation or an impending situation that constitutes a danger of major proportion that could result in serious harm to persons or substantial damage to property that is caused by the forces of nature, a disease or other health hazard, an accident or an act whether intentional or otherwise." (Barrie, Ontario)

> - "A central focal point of analytical and coordinative planning skills which could obtain the necessary political leadership and backing when needed, is required to coordinate the program and agencies necessary to bring about a high quality level of recovery and community redevelopment." (Buffalo, New York)
>
> - "Conflagration is defined as a fire incident with a front of at least 300 feet or when a fire has jumped across a natural barrier." (Austin, Texas)

Oklahoma City explains, under its "High Winds" category, that "wind is defined as the motion of air relative to the earth's surface." Later the same plan states: "Hazardous materials are essential to the economy of the United States and the well being of its people." This may well be true, but is more appropriate for a corporate, or Board of Trade booster pamphlet than an emergency plan. There's also a section that goes into great detail about the 10-step methodology by which the plan was made, none of which has any relevance once an emergency strikes. No wonder this plan runs to over 350 pages!

Interestingly, the 10-step methodology includes a detailed and comprehensive cycle of organization, public consultation, coordination, hazard assessment, problem evaluation, goal setting, reviewing mitigation strategies, drafting an action plan, adopting the plan, and finally plan maintenance. The cycle is structured to allow for constant re-cycling of steps 2–10 so the plan is up to date. Then another chapter goes into exactly how each step is to be reviewed and re-evaluated. However it appears nobody has heeded this part of the plan. It hasn't been updated since 2006.

San Diego County's plan runs to more than 450 pages. More than 100 pages are devoted to assessing the risk of possible hazards, and another 300 pages on outlining goals and objectives. Much of the remainder is spent describing the role of various emergency management personnel.

The Australian city of Brisbane, divides its plan into several 'shorter' plans. The first 40 or so pages outline the city's profile, birth rate, indigenous population, vocational education and training institutions. These shorter plans range from 10–40 pages, each with its own executive summary and a page of acronyms at the end. The document runs to more than 200 pages.

In the event of a crisis, every second can be the difference between lives lost and lives saved. Emergency plans with navigational difficulties, convoluted language, acronyms and jargon waste valuable time. A long plan gets worse if there is a poorly constructed table of contents, small font, and abstract definitions.

Some things, however, deserve more explanation. Nine of the city plans I reviewed inadequately explained important categories and instructions. Brisbane often refers to "lead agencies" in recovery efforts. Although various agencies that work for the city are listed, there is no way to differentiate which is considered "lead." St. Catharines, Ontario, says the job of the Emergency Information Officer (EIO) is to "correct misinformation by contacting media program producers." It doesn't explain how the EIO will know the information is incorrect, or where and how he finds the right information. This direction also leaves out newspapers, social media and small radio and TV stations which may not have program producers.

Two Canadian cities (Calgary and St. Catharines) often refer to something "as defined in annex." Yet parts or all of the annexes are hidden or missing from the public plan. Another city, Seattle, didn't explain how "electric buses will be used to provide power." Will the bus be using its own power or carrying portable sources of power? These are crucial details that are worth defining, and will matter when the moment calls for them. Finding out how buses will provide power during a power outage, weather event or terrorism event will not be easy. Plans should clearly state what capabilities exist.

# Crisis Plans – A Closer Look

My critique of these plans is not to minimize the effort that their writers made. It is more a commentary on the lack of coordination within the response community. This not only means the documented different approaches that different response organizations have (police, fire, EMS, military) within the same city, but also significant differences within a single response organization in neighbouring jurisdictions.

I've singled out Baltimore's plan to help highlight the challenges we face in planning for large–scale emergencies in urban areas. I read this plan in the hopes of obtaining specific information about the use of transit during evacuations, but found little. However, it did contain some things of value we can use as we confront the challenges and search for solutions.

### Solutions, Not Problems

The solution to some problems can be simpler than some plans imply. It may not require discussion by committees, new planning, budgets or laws, but arrived at with common sense or individual actions. Sometimes solutions can be found in the description of the problem or in discussion of a different problem.

Baltimore's plan cites the hazard of "Extreme Heat," among many others. This regular condition is exacerbated by "large, uninterrupted stretches of hardscape (sidewalks,

***City Hall's Podium Green Roof, Toronto.***
*Built to showcase the city's commitment to the environment, the green roof replaced concrete and reduced the building's environmental impact, while allowing workers, residents and visitors a relaxing and rejuvenating slice of nature in the heart of the city.*

flooding *and* extreme heat. Planners could encourage green roofs and walls where possible and rooftop gardens where safe. Even window boxes or plants on balconies would help. So would painting roofs white. Of greater help would be the increased use of honeycombed hard tiles for driveways with slow growing grass in each hole. Large civic and shopping centre parking lots can be made from these tiles and landscaped with species of trees which consume less water than average.

While discussing the extreme heat hazard Baltimore's plan tells us that "[o]lder residents remember sleeping on rooftops or in parks to obtain relief from the heat. Today these options are seen by most residents in most of Baltimore as unsafe." It's hard to imagine very many cities in which residents feel safe sleeping in parks and given changes over the years in building codes and styles it's hard to imagine people venturing onto their roofs for any reason. Most roofs wouldn't conform to code for any use, let alone sleeping.

By the same token, it's not at all hard to imagine addressing both of these issues. Knowing the challenge of heat, the number and kind of housing stock and the disadvantaged population without air conditioning, there could be a by–law written to outline the ways and means of retrofitting some roofs for recreation and even sleeping. There could even be grants or loans for retrofitting and greening roofs. In short, why not make sleeping outdoors and on rooftops safe?

buildings, streets, etc.)," which makes downtown hotter than surrounding areas and occurs "nearly every summer." A few pages later it suggests a solution: "To 'green' Baltimore" with trees, grass and so on. Elsewhere in the plan readers are told the city also has a problem with flooding due to rain storms. This too is exacerbated by hardscape. Now we have two problems caused by paving over grass and soil – extreme heat and flooding.

Common sense suggests that making hardscape less hard so that it absorbs more water will reduce the risk of

There are ways to make sleeping in parks safe. Even if parks were not often used for sleeping, safety is a worthy goal itself and should be pursued. But, what if the city had a 'summer sleepover,' campaign involving the boy and girl scouts? Several weekends could be designated for pitching tents and sleeping under supervision, including with parents. The police could patrol. City services including medical, public works, fire and others could have displays that appeal to the Boy and Girl Scouts' ethic to 'be prepared.'

What this program would do is allow average citizens to take back their parks in a controlled and safe way. Then, in a heat emergency vulnerable people could get a respite in their parks safely. In fact, if the use of air conditioners were threatening to cause a brown or black out, the city could invoke summer sleepover and even start it at noon Friday or give the kids a full day off school to take the pressure off home and school air conditioning systems.

*Tents in Confederation Park, Ottawa.*
*The Occupy movement's use of public spaces as temporary housing created public debates about the appropriate uses of parkland in the city. Creating programs to make sleepovers in public parks in warm weather commonplace might make us better able to deal with electricity shortages.*

## Navigation and Clarity

The printed hard copy of the Baltimore plan that I have is badly formatted. The opening sentence tells me that "Baltimore City Announces Participation in....." and the line ends there. Words in each sentence are clipped off so I can only guess at the meaning. Electronic interactivity is lost on the printed page, of course. But interactive elements often obscure other features on the paper page. Text is interrupted and can't be read because of what appears to be a pop–up or drop–down menu reading "Citywide Menu" and another entitled "Select Language." Some maps are so small they are illegible. Others maps obscure text. No maps that I can see have street names, titles or cut lines to describe what I'm looking at.

To be fair there is a notation that "This page contains links to files which may require additional software to view." But, the ability to download "free viewers below" is useless on paper. Responders who decide to print out the plan will have difficulty making sense of some parts and in a power outage they won't be able fill in the gaps.

There are good reasons to have clear, printable maps in crisis plans. We have all been temporarily lost in a cab or in our own cars even in our home towns. There are occasional tragic stories of EMS vehicles going to the wrong address after a 911 call because of similar or identical street names. Not all streets and intersections have signs, and some parts of a street will have different names. Clear,

legible printed maps are essential – hence our ranking of the maps in emergency plans (see appendix) is based on the availability of readable and printable maps.

Both a lack of clarity and protracted or 'hyper' clarity can be equally problematic. In the Baltimore plan, significant lines of text are used to define the obvious:

- "Winter storms are large storms occurring during the cold, winter months."

- "Droughts simply are extended periods of dry weather."

- "Flooding occurs when rivers, creeks, streams, ditches, or other water bodies receive too much water from rain or snowmelt."

- "Hail is a large frozen raindrop..."

Those who download and print the plan also receive eight pages containing the names of the local emergency planning committee. But since the plan is 10 years old, many must have moved on, and some may have died. Regardless, knowing who is present, absent or dead will surely not help the average citizen, business or institution to be more prepared.

## All Hazard Plans

In order to qualify for disaster assistance from the federal government in Washington, planners in the US must follow guidelines set out by the Federal Emergency Management Agency (FEMA). These include a stipulation that emergency plans must address "all hazards." Baltimore's plan uses the term Emergency Support Function (ESF) to describe a service or set of services likely to be required during a wide range of incidents.

The notion of a plan that has response elements and capabilities which can be effective in a variety of incidents is a good one. Clients often ask me if I will help them list all possible emergencies which may befall them. While there is some value in this, the far greater value is in compiling a list of all possible response capabilities that might be needed. This is a better use of resources.

If you list all the possible emergencies you might face and then list all the possible solutions, you might be tempted to list all the centimetres of snow that might fall and construct a plan listing the number and kind of trucks required to address each increment in snowfall. Isn't it better to have a full inventory of available heavy equipment such as ploughs, graders, front–end loaders, dump trucks and so on? It is irrelevant whether these are normally used in farming, road building, mining or other applications. The point of the inventory is to be able to call on this equipment should a need arise. The all hazards aspect involves the fact that this equipment will be helpful in a road washout, land-slide, rock fall, sink hole, sandstorm, storm which deposits debris on shore and perhaps in many other events, which probably can't be anticipated and listed. This is what Baltimore's ESFs should list – capabilities not problems.

An anecdote may illustrate this point. An acquaintance of mine, the late Charles Gaines, was second to arrive at the Murrah Federal Building in Oklahoma City. Charles was the Deputy Fire Chief responding to a call. When he looked at the building, he thought it was a false alarm – everything looked just fine. But when he walked around to the other side, he saw a huge swath cut out of the structure – exposing open floors of office space to the elements.

His first thought was that a plane had crashed into the building. Not having a response plan for a plane crashing into a building, the fire department invoked its tornado plan. The point being that an explosion, tornado or plane might cause very similar damage. An explosion could be accidental or purposeful. The explosive could be in a gas main, device in a suitcase or rental truck and could be farmers' dynamite or nitroglycerine.

It is of little consequence to the dead and injured just why the explosion happened. It is of little consequence to responders. Response is much the same, regardless of cause. Responders need food, the injured need medical attention and rubble needs to be searched. In the case of vandalism or terrorism, bad people have to be pursued.

Once it was determined that a bomb had caused the damage in Oklahoma City, response remained the same.

A complicating factor with terrorism is the potential for a planned second explosion designed to kill and injure responders and evacuees. This didn't happen in Oklahoma City. What did change response was finding that the FBI had stored a number of weapons, including explosives in the Federal Building. When fire fighters discovered this, they ran out until it was safe to continue.

In the end, we must put out fires regardless of the cause. This is the essence of ESFs. We have a water supply to douse flames, regardless of how the fire started. We respond to emergencies no matter what caused them.

Oddly though, in Baltimore's "all hazards plan" there is also an evaluation of "the frequency and magnitude of different hazards." In fact, there's far more about potential hazards than actual response techniques. The plan also quotes FEMA as requiring "a comprehensive range of mitigation actions for each hazard identified." This appears to be the opposite of the ESF and all hazards strategy. When the task of writing a plan is passed down the line or divided among officials, a great deal of time can be taken up writing under conflicting direction or assembling extraneous material.

The plan writers of Baltimore have actually gone to some trouble to list and quantify hazards, many of which don't exist. For example, they considered "avalanche" as a hazard. But a "Lack of mountainous terrain makes hazard improbable." The same is true of "Volcano." Plan writers conducted an interview with Geological Survey officials and determined that the volcano "hazard does not

significantly affect Baltimore." This (tautologically) is a result of no volcanic mountains being present.

Thoughtful people often do the right thing around their homes. They lock the doors without having a long family discussion about just who might use an unlocked door and why. We ask our children to look both ways before crossing the street – a direction which is more valuable than a discussion about whether a truck, car, motorcycle driven by a young, old or impaired person might strike the child. The essence of emergency planning and response is action, not contemplating causes.

### Private Sector Plans

Perhaps the most motivating experience I've had in this field occurred when I was asked to review a multinational mining company's crisis plans. You may think that the private sector, with money at stake, might do better at crisis planning than the public sector with only the last political leader's reputation at stake. I've found it ain't necessarily so.

The mining company's plans were on a secure website. With the appropriate code I began downloading the English–language versions covering its global operations. This took 17 hours and wore out at least one toner cartridge. To state the obvious: Many crises would either be over or well out of control in that space of time. I could just as easily have run out of ink and paper with such a large print job. And if I had to drive or fly to reach an isolated mine in crisis, I'd be leaving with only half the plan printed out.

Once the plans for my mining client were printed, I had a view of the broad corporate approach to crisis management that a planner in an individual location might not. First, while banal on first thought, formatting issues seemed very important in the end. Some location plans were in Word format, some in WordPerfect and others were saved in PDF. Printing, editing or collating could have been a problem in a crisis. Some plans had Roman numerals, others Arabic numbers and still others had lettering to signify page order. In the end, it was difficult to know a page 'I' from a page '1' or an 'II' from an '11' or an '11.'

However, there were far more important issues than formatting. Two could have created very serious problems. In parts of Africa, car-jacking and kidnappings are a significant threat. In any jurisdiction I would have expected a note of caution about executive safety, but I was shocked to find the applicable section for South Africa contained just two instructions:

- Retain a local lawyer to negotiate with the hostage takers
- Obtain a volunteer employee to deliver ransom

It seems obvious that both could make a hostage taking worse and both would endanger at least two additional people. Hostage negotiation is a skill and it's hard to imagine being able to find a lawyer with this skill in a remote jurisdiction on short notice. Delivering ransom puts someone in close contact with the hostage takers who may have motives other than money. They may be terrorists with spreading terror as their simple goal, or activists with revenge on their minds. Both matters should be left to professionals trained in the appropriate areas of expertise.

I reported my findings to head office. Ironically, head office had been unaware of the local stipulation. This is a result of crisis plans lingering on shelves or being updated by several people over time with no central oversight. Doubly ironically, I was told that head office had a standing retainer with a counter-terrorism unit in London, ready to respond to just such an incident at any of the company's mines anywhere in the world. Obviously this information had not been adequately disseminated within the company.

*Communicating Useful Information*
Obviously warning people in a timely manner then advising them what to do and how to do it is vital. With an extended power outage, or with a sleeping population, traditional forms of communication such as broadcast radio and television will not be very effective. Unfortunately these two

are the most common approaches I found cities to be using in the emergency plans I reviewed. A better method of communication is direct notification by text message or email updates, which residents can sign up for. Unfortunately many cities I reviewed lack such a system.

We should also remember that the benefits of direct–notification systems will disappear if batteries are dead or the internet is down – common occurrences in extended power outages. A few cities have taken the trouble to explore other methods to communicate information to the public during a crisis. Leeds, in England, plans to use 'sky shout' where police helicopters deliver messages via loud-speakers. Detroit will use emergency vehicles on the road to deliver messages over loudspeakers. Both Dallas and Fort Worth have installed emergency sirens in neighbour-hoods near bodies of water or which are prone to weather–related disasters such as hurricanes.

Even the best prepared emergency response plans will have limited impact if they are locked away in a cupboard or desk or otherwise hidden from view. As we move ever closer to a paperless society, we look for information on-line, in likely websites. Most of the 100 cities we surveyed had used websites to display emergency preparedness information for their citizens. However, searching for specific information on these sites was as difficult as looking in different cupboards, desks and draws in different offices. Information was fragmented and links were hard to find.

Glasgow, for example, does not have a single path to finding out how to deal with various problems associated with an emergency. First you have to search for a link to floods, for example. Then if you are concerned about a re-sulting power outage you have to begin searching for another link. And then a different link for preparing a 'go bag.' Unless you have spent time on this site, finding all these extra links takes time – maybe more time than would be available in a real emergency. Some cities have eased this problem by creating a comprehensive emergency plan for households that can be downloaded, printed and reviewed periodically.

### The Growth of Social Media

Recently we've seen the growing reach of social media and everybody involved, or interested in planning for large scale emergencies in their communities needs to be aware of it.

Even users of social media might be tempted to dis-count any useful role it might play in emergency response. Twitter, Facebook, Instagram and other so–called 'channels' of communication seem to have facilitated the instant global exchange of humdrum messages of little interest and even less importance. And yet we do know that social media has played a role in major events around the world in recent years – though not always a constructive one.

Legacy or old media (radio, TV & print) appear to have more substantial and filtered or edited information. But on closer examination, old media have always had to appeal to a wide audience and hence the term 'broadcasting' for electronic media. Old media will report an event in a region, section of a city or county, but not usually define that area specifically by streets or grid (or concession) roads. If news consumers have a cursory interest in that region, this general information may be interesting. However, if loved ones are lost, toxic gas released or if there's an evacuation order, citizens need more specific information.

Similarly, news on old or legacy media is not usually 'new.' There are so many sources of information that broadcast media and newspapers are usually behind the reporting to be found on 'all news' stations, speciality and cable talk shows. They are also increasingly behind social media.

All media or channels of communication feature 'noise.' There are features, human interest or undated stories on traditional newscasts, which one consumes along with the hard news of the day. There are commentators and backgrounders on all news and talk channels. This is roughly akin to the noise on social media – cats, personal information and repeats of old media content. Noise is unimportant information, filler or 'infotainment.'

There is a case to be made that the characteristics of social media are more useful in a crisis than those of legacy media. In short, the noise is vastly reduced. The content becomes very specific, emergency–oriented and more timely than the content of old media. Social media may be the best source of information about the whereabouts of a fire, toxic cloud or other potential danger. The information is more timely as well. There are exceptions and flaws, but we appear to be at the beginning of an era in which social media will be among the most valuable resources for emergency responders and citizens. Hence our ranking of city emergency plans which appear to be trying to take full advantage of these new tools (see appendix).

In order to understand more fully the importance of social media, it's best to start with how pervasive these tools are. In 2010, nearly 80% of all Canadians had internet access, and according to a Leger Marketing survey carried out with the participation of Canadian Heritage between November 2010 and April 2011. The biggest reason most people (nearly 60%) gave for their use of the Internet was to access social networks. These figures are increasing yearly.

The Print Measurement Bureau provides other telling data. Social media 'networkers' are defined as those visiting two or more different social media websites within a given month. About 13 million Canadians, or 59% of those aged 12 and above, are social media networkers. Approximately one–third of these networkers are under 25 years of age, and almost six out of ten are under 35. There's about an equal gender split among social media networkers. Speakers of English (60%) are more likely to be social media networkers than Francophones (49%). An emergency planner wanting to reach Canadians would do well to use these data.

There are similar data in America, where the Pew Research Centre reports that 33% of adults under 30 get their news from social media. Interestingly, it also found that Twitter users connect more with journalists and news organizations than with other social networks. News organizations and journalists encourage these followers and some journalists have Tweeting and blogging activities mandated in their contracts.

Pew data also show how important smart phones could be during a crisis. Ninety per cent of 18–29 year olds say they sleep with their phones in or right next to their beds. That provides a good way to communicate with them during an emergency – providing they have sufficient battery power and that service is available.

According to a report from Google, 56% of Canadian adults were using smart phones in 2013, up from 33% in 2012. Almost 80% of them said they also used social media and more than half said they logged on daily.

Of all the social media, Twitter appears best suited for rapid information dissemination and communication. Compared to Facebook and email, Twitter is the most immediate. 'Conversations' happen instantly, and users have multiple conversations simultaneously.

When Calgary, Alberta, experienced massive flooding for three weeks during June and July 2013, Twitter logged more than 850,000 tweets. The city's government and police force had the most re–tweets, indicating that 'official sources' garnered the most attention. In particular, the mayor's prolific tweeting considerably enhanced his reputation and popularity.

A study by the Canadian Red Cross, found that 33% of the population would call for help using social media, although it is not really set up to handle such calls. At least one police force which uses social media as an information source cautions that it's not a reporting mechanism for the police. Skype features a similar disclaimer. Nonetheless, almost half all Canadians say they'll "sign up" for social media information from response organizations. At the same time the Red Cross calls social media an important "crowd source" of crisis information and points to the ability to "geomap" events and locations of problems.

As transit companies use Twitter and other platforms to spread information about changes in schedules or service disruptions, commuters will become more used to obtaining and using this kind of information. New automobiles are now outfitted to handle this information as well. All of this is a good reason for emergency planners to factor social media into their plans (see appendix).

Of course, social media isn't perfect. In the aftermath of the earthquake and tsunami that struck Japan in 2011, some victims were able to tweet for help when emergency phone lines were jammed or disabled. However there were also cases of tweets for help being re–tweeted long after the original sender had been located and rescued.

After the Boston Marathon bombing of April 2013, social media identified a student who had been missing for weeks as one of the suspects. In a matter of hours his name had been spread around the world both by social and some mainstream media that felt under pressure to compete with Twitter and Reddit. The information was unsubstantiated and wrong.

Furthermore, there are those who would use social media to increase their reach for improper or illegal purposes. The potential for terrorists to use social media to spread disinformation is a major concern. A common terror technique is to set off a small explosion to help stampede people into an area where more bombs are waiting.

Nevertheless, it's clear these information channels are here to stay and people involved in planning for emergencies may be able to make use of them in all sorts of ways. One academic study from Boston's Northeastern University is optimistic about several roles for social media in emergency planning and response. It sees social media users as a potential for "massive data sets" for study and suggests entire populations could be used as "social sensors." Some public health researchers are already monitoring key words (flu, fear, sick) to see if this will provide early alerts to outbreaks, epidemics and pandemics. Tweets about earth tremors may alert citizens and responders to earthquakes far faster than scientific instruments can.

## A Question Of Transport

While transport obviously must play a major role in any community's emergency plan, our review of plans and follow-up questionnaire revealed a surprising shortage of hard data and curious gaps in knowledge and experience.

Diesel-powered buses appear to dominate transport systems, although there are also electric-hybrids and probably gasoline-powered buses too. Some cities and transit systems have their own supply of fuel. However, it is unclear whether they also maintain stockpiles of fuel in case of emergency, whether those stockpiles can be accessed easily during an emergency and which vehicles would have priority during an emergency. Since it would not be practical to transport people out of town and then return to refuel it would be interesting to know if there's a capability for refuelling depots along evacuation routes.

On the fundamental question regarding how many residents can be moved by transit at any given time, there were few clear answers. We suspect many were guesses. For example, according to the City of Thunder Bay, on the shores of Lake Superior, only 2% of its residents are in that category – yet 50% of those living in areas adjoining the city could be moved. There could be several reasons for this huge discrepancy in numbers but we are left to guess.

The large number of less-than-specific answers and the number of times we were referred to transit authorities in the hopes of getting this information lead us to conclude that insufficient thought has been given to evacuating cities with the help of transit vehicles. Indeed a US federal study concurs, indicating that transit and evacuation are largely ignored in civic emergency plans and that evacuation is a "significant weakness." An acquaintance of mine, Canadian researcher Joe Scanlon, concurs, writing that transport and evacuation are "often overlooked" in emergency planning.

Particularly worrisome is the reliance on outside agencies for answers. Of course it makes sense that transit authorities should be best informed about their capabilities, but how can officials who are planning responses to emergencies not be aware of the assets at their disposal?

We received some answers that fall into the category of wishful thinking, or what some studies call "fantasy plans." The notion that "contra flow," the practice of reversing the flow of one or more lanes of traffic on major routes to speed up evacuation, can be introduced at short notice without causing chaos is one example. So is the belief that emergency vehicles will be able to operate normally on clogged evacuation routs. So is the reliance on private cars. Some cities have plans to use water taxis in evacuations, but there's no information on how many there are, or how many people they accommodate – or even if they exist.

However, we also found some interesting ideas along with a few refreshingly candid admissions of concern:

- Sault Ste. Marie plans to use wheelchair accessible cabs for those with mobility issues

- Ottawa notes that the coaches it uses for highway commuters (as opposed to inner city buses) can't accommodate wheelchairs and hopes that family members will provide assistance

- Coquitlam admits frankly that it doesn't have a plan to help those with mobility issues

- San Jose bluntly warns that in the event of a catastrophic earthquake it may not be able to move any of its residents

### Some Background

As part of our review of emergency preparedness for 100 cities in the mainly English–speaking world, we sought additional information from their emergency mangers. We communicated with 87 North American cities by telephone and email and with cities in Australia, New Zealand and the UK by email only.

For the North American cities, we began with a telephone call to the city emergency manger if that number was available on the website or to the city's general number if a specific number for that person was not. We found that 30 out of 87 cities publish a specific number for the emergency manager prominently. We called them all.

We reached 27 on the first phone call, with most being transferred by a receptionist. All but one provided an email address on this first call. We left voice mail for another 54 and were given email addresses for five of them by their receptionists. There was no answer from one and that email address was also unobtainable.

Within 33 days of our initial contacts, we received return phone calls from 26 additional emergency responders: 34 of 87 mangers with a mandate to communicate about public safety in their cities did not respond to phone calls.

We followed up with emails and after 50 days we had a total of 45 email addresses. We sent a questionnaire to all of them and eventually received 14 back, one of which was incomplete (see appendix).

The paucity of the responses we received may or may not tell a story about preparedness in the cities in question. It is entirely possible that an emergency manager may be excellent at this function, but not willing or able to participate in surveys. It may be that this person feels no duty to callers who are citizens of another community. But it may also indicate that many city emergency managers don't see any need to interact with citizens of their own communities who wish to become more prepared for an emergency.

Sometimes important lessons are hidden in the apparent findings of research. For example the fact that about 20% of Canadians don't use the Internet is equally or more interesting than the fact that 80% do. Similarly, the fact that we could only obtain a response of about 20% (including detailed refusals or responses questioning our motivation) is noteworthy. This seemingly low response was after at least two contacts – phone and email over several weeks. This low response was from a study group or population with either a legislated mandate for public education or a fiduciary duty to educate.

Certainly a better prepared and educated public will tend to make the emergency managers' jobs easier.

We recognize that city administrations have hierarchies and divisions of labour, and that civic employees receive regular inquiries from the public. But when I was on the political staff of the world's longest serving big city Mayor, responding to an inquiry from the public was mandatory. I've also found that the police, fire, ambulance and other paramilitary and emergency response people I've encountered are 'can do' people so I was expecting a higher rate and better quality of response.

I was struck by the incurious nature of most responders. There is a concept called 'management by walking around.' Police and private security guards display curiosity, as do journalists. The fact that most responders seemed unaware of basic facts about their transit systems, contra flow, pathways, journalists working city hall, signage and so on is noteworthy. One assumes these facts are available down the hall from colleagues at city hall or in regular round table preparedness meetings.

We received a number of responses which were not to the question asked:

Q: Do you receive many calls asking for help in getting more prepared?

A: We exercise our emergency plan on a regular basis and have an exercise schedule

Q: Does your physical setting lend itself to creative transport modes such as ski gondolas, ferries and so on?

A ...We work closely with our partners in _____ (a neighbouring city)

Q: Do you have/use signs indicating direction and mileage to areas that may be safer in an emergency?

A: All information ... will be communicated through multiple media channels..."

To critique is not necessarily to be critical. There are reasons to be positive about urban crisis planning. The use of multiple languages and videos is a case in point – recognizing the reality of our multicultural population and the pervasiveness of video. Some cities have multiple, good quality videos on a range of topics. The use of social media is promising. We can only classify it as an experiment until response organizations take the lead and help develop the optimum use of this tool. Moreover, technology is moving so quickly, some social media cited in this book may be replaced by others shortly. Within the small group of emergency managers who responded, we found a reasonable effort to communicate with the public. Before a final observation can be made, I'd want to test whether these efforts have changed attitudes or behaviour.

# Conclusion

It is difficult for us not to be concerned – if not downright scared – about our urban futures when we are stuck regularly in never–ending traffic jams, or trapped between stations on a commuter train above or below ground because of service disruptions. Our anxiety level increases if we happen to live in a location subject to extremes of weather, where our next 'natural' disaster could be only a season away.

I've tried to show that it is only prudent for us to take stock of our situation(s) so that we are better prepared to handle the challenges we may have to face in the future – if not tomorrow, then perhaps five or ten years from now when our urban populations have expanded considerably.

Planning for the future isn't always easy but it has to be easier in our 'developed' world than anywhere else. Compared to the difficulties facing the rest of the world we have little to complain about and our challenges are marginal.

As noted earlier, the world's population seems to be stampeding into cities. As of 2014 the world had 30 megacities with populations exceeding 10 million. However, 11 of them are actually hypercities with more than 20 million residents. One of them – Tokyo – has a population of 38 million, which is greater than Canada's!

However, the fastest growth in urban populations is not in the developed world but in the less developed countries of Asia and Africa. Here are some revealing statistics from the United Nations in its 2014 report on the World's Urbanization Prospects:

- 54 per cent of the world's population live in urban areas. This is expected to rise to 66 per cent by 2050 with close to 90 percent of the increase concentrated in Asia and Africa

- The largest urban growth will take place in India, China and Nigeria. These three countries will account for 37 per cent of the projected growth of the world's urban population between 2014 and 2050

- By 2050, the world's urban population will exceed six billion people

Without proper planning, most of these fast–growing megacities probably will end up as megaslums. According to John Wilmoth, Director of the Population Division in the UN's Department of Economic and Social Affairs: "Managing urban areas has become one of the most important development challenges of the 21st century."

In our less urbanized world of today, the World Health Organization reports that more than 2.6 billion people (that's half the population of the developing world) don't have access to basic sanitation.

In addition, a similar number don't have access to modern fuels; about two million people die each year from inhaling the smoke of cooking fires (most of them are children). It's been estimated that people spend 50 billion hours a year collecting firewood to burn and the resulting degradation of habitat and atmosphere create more challenges.

These killer challenges are magnified when they take root in urban settings but their impacts are not limited to the poor. A recent report by UN–Habitat, the United Nations program aimed at improving human settlements, warns:

*"A quasi universal steepening of social inequities is taking on a particularly serious dimension in cities where extreme affluence can be found side by side with great poverty within restricted areas, in the process generating social instability and insecurity, with huge economic and social costs not just for the underprivileged but for the whole of society, too. The majority of urban populations come under a diversity of constraints of an economic, social, cultural and environmental nature. In many developing countries, urban growth has frequently been characterised by the informal and/or illegal nature of human settlements, a clear demonstration of the failure of urban policies. This urban growth has been strongly associated with greater poverty and slum expansion."*

The report goes on to note that some progress is being made. Between 2000 and 2010, governments of developing

(poor) countries managed to significantly improve the living conditions of 227 million slum dwellers. Unfortunately the rapid growth of cities in Asia and Africa means that by 2020 the actual number of slum dwellers will be closer to 900 million.

For most of us the problems confronting the poorest parts of the world are far away. Foreign aid and assistance are never at the top of any government's agenda, and when our own economies are stagnating or in decline that aid and assistance is pushed even lower. We don't need Hollywood to scare us with imaginary scenarios if our world continues on this downward path. Just look at today's news coverage.

In North America we see a never–ending stream of economic refugees heading across Central America in the hopes of a better life in the US. European countries bordering the Mediterranean are dealing with thousands of boat people fleeing Africa, and Australia is worrying about boatloads of refugees from Asia.

If we, in our privileged lives, find ourselves overwhelmed by the challenges we face in our growing cities, imagine the feelings of helplessness of people in the mega and hypercities of Asia and Africa.

But here again, perhaps the only way forward is to take small steps to chip away at the big picture until it becomes more manageable.

What follows are a few ideas that have already emerged to help improve life in the most desperate slums.

### Sanitation

Even the developed world experiences problems in this area. While viewing my neighbourhood close to downtown Toronto from a high–rise I can see that alleyways (and sometimes rooftops) make convenient latrines for homeless people and others, who occasionally feel their needs trump social manners and hygiene.

Public toilets are common in Europe but not so common in North America, where we tend to rely on shopping malls, public buildings and transportation hubs to provide the necessary facilities.

Sanitation in the world's new megacities and hyper cities presents much greater challenges. A rapid influx of people into newly–urbanized areas creates illegal, unplanned and unserviced neighbourhoods. In Nairobi's slums there is just one toilet for every 150 people. But improvements can be made.

In Indore, India, they are installing experimental storm drainage, water and sewer hookups, solid waste management and other services. These improvements may end up being temporary but they are having a tangible and psychological effect on the lives of people in these fragile communities.

Students from the Massachusetts Institute of Technology have formed a company called Sanergy which is building toilets for about $200 each. They are selling them to people in Nairobi who become franchisees for a fee of $6.25 per month. Users pay six cents a visit and the biogas is used to generate electricity. The MIT students call this "the sanitation value chain."

Also in Nairobi, multi–story BioCentres convert human waste into fertilizer and methane for cooking and heating water. These facilities provide toilets and showers at little cost.

### Water

Potable water is an issue all over the world. Diarrhoea kills more people than any other disease, more than 1,500 per day. Much of the diarrhoea problem is a result of unclean water. In addition to the water issue hitting poor people in undeveloped regions the hardest, it also hits women the hardest. They are usually the ones with family responsibilities for cooking and cleaning.

There has been progress on the margins on the water and food issue. Segregating animals from the human water supply produces good results. So do covering wells and using culverts to prevent run–off and contamination.

The Q Drum is a hollow water wheel which can be filled with 50 litres of water. This is too heavy to lift, but it can be rolled or pulled. Manually operated pumps and gravity fed systems can assist as well. There are systems

which allow human power to access water several feet down for irrigation and the Bamboo Treadle Pump (like a first–world elliptical machine) does the same with a mechanical advantage. Almost two million have been sold in Bangladesh, generating almost one and a half million dollars in farmer income.

One of the simplest ways of making water potable is with chlorine. A new simple dispenser, installed near communal drinking supplies, is allowing people to treat their water with the correct dose of chlorine after they fill jerrycans and other containers. The cost is less than thirty cents per person per year.

AquaStar Plus has developed a water bottle that exposes the water to UV–C light which damages the DNA and RNA in pathogens. Meanwhile a Guatemalan chemist has developed a ceramic water filter which combines the filtration capability of ceramics with the anti–bacterial quality of colloidal silver. About a half a million people have used the product redesigned by Potters for Peace. A gravity fed system developed in Chile uses an elevated storage tank that is filled by a foot pump. More portable still is the LifeStraw – a personal water–purification tool that can be carried easily and used to turn any surface water into safe drinking water.

*Energy*

Few things better symbolize the gulf between between rich and poor countries than the amount of energy consumed by their respective populations. Consider the relatively simple challenge we face in finding a convenient power point to re–charge a cell phone, iPad or tablet. Hypercity slum dwellers may need cell phones to locate work opportunities but have to travel considerable distances on foot to access power and, may face a threat from thieves and gangs along the way. Here again, there are small solutions.

One company, Tellurex Corporation, has found a way to use the steam from a kettle on an open fire to power an electric generator to charge phones or other devices. In another development, Internet Village Motoman uses five Honda motorcycles to power a satellite uplink to connect 15 village schools, medical clinics and the governor's office in a remote part of Cambodia. There are also a system that uses the pedal power of bicycles to re–charge cell phones. It's an adaptation of the old dynamo friction generator that powered front and rear bicycle lights.

*Small v. Big*

Small solutions and actions may alleviate big problems in the fast growing urban areas of poor countries but it is hard to see how they might solve them in the long term. What they need is long–term political and economic stability and in most cases that seems a very long way off. But what is our objection to using smaller solutions to tackle the less serious problems we face in the cities of the developed world? A possible reason is that we all take pride in our individuality and are wary of joining in mass or large scale community actions that we fear might have a negative affect on our neighbourhoods under the guise of 'improving' them.

While activists like to stress the need for community spirit and cohesion to press for and achieve common goals, it can be extremely difficult to find agreement on what those goals should be: Subways? Better roads? More parks? Eco–friendly initiatives? They all cost money and these days politicians who are honest enough to point out that initiatives will probably increase the community's tax load are not very popular.

Life in densely packed urban areas requires us to surrender at least some of our personal space and attempt to get along with our neighbours – even if we don't see them as friends. If there's a way forward to achieve better and safer cities we have to build on that.

## Conclusion

Now let's go back to where we began – my city. Is there an example there that can help make all cities better? I believe so.

We're in the midst of multiple debates about how to make our city work better. Ideas include tearing down the elevated expressway, subways, surface subways, more buses, toll roads, toll zones, commuter ferries, light rail on underused railway tracks, and my favourites – elevated transit including trams, sky trains and monorails. I'm increasingly hearing well-informed planners advocating building every transit system possible, because we'll probably need each and every one. Even if driverless cars and telecommuting drastically reduce the number of people on the move in our cities, we'll still have congestion and pollution without drastic action.

And what of the cost? We think little about the cost of the world's first fully retractible domed stadium being budgeted at $150 million, costing almost $600 million in the end and being sold for $25 million to the private sector. Vancouver's BC Place cost about as much to renovate and some American stadiums cost more. These are considered necessary civic amenities – an entry into the big leagues.

Subways have probably had their day because of cost. New railway tracks tie us to light or heavy rail. But using existing tracks or overhead wires, our existing waterway and our streets for buses and surface subways (long, articulated buses on dedicated lanes) is forgivable public policy.

The expenditure won't be a waste because the transport system can be used elsewhere if future population growth doesn't support it. Regardless, we'll have cleaner air and better evacuation plans.

And what of the developing world – or perhaps that part of the world that doesn't seem to have much hope of developing? Foreign aid doesn't seem to be a reliable fix since we keep hearing stories of money disappearing into a dictator's private bank account. Aid in kind harnesses the legitimate self-interest of people in the developed world who make something of value to the developing world. At least there's some clean water, firewood conservation or sanitation at the end of the process.

Capitalism has a tremendous capacity to foster growth and innovation. If bicycle-mounted phone, computer and tablet chargers become the vogue in Amsterdam, Portland and Copenhagen where there are lots of bicyclists, innovation will follow. The devices will become more efficient and smaller. If those cities pass a bylaw to mandate a new generation of these devices, the older models could be given as aid in kind to the developing world with some good results.

This innovation cycle could work for potable water, sanitation, food safety, heating and many other life and death issues. That's in the short term. But what of the long-term for the mega-cities and mega-slums?

Is the solution to life and death issues really to have students at Ivy League schools compete for a prize for

*Portland Aerial Tram, Portland.*
*Built to connect both the riverside and mountain campuses of the Oregon Health & Science University, the tram is now a popular attraction. As our urban regions continue to swell, can we avoid introducing innovative solutions to old problems?*

making the cheapest toilet or phone charger? Is it turning desperate people into entrepreneurs who charge a few cents to enter a pay toilet? Is it feeling good in the developed world because we're letting desperate people drive hand–me–down bicycles and appliances in need of repair? What will that do in the long–term to relieve the tension between the haves and have–nots?

I'm all for short–term solutions – water, sanitation, sound farming techniques and so on. But we also need long–term, structural solutions that work where the people who need them live. Tens of millions of people on the move in the world, seeking a better life, is not sustainable. If this book has raised some issues and pointed to the need to make life better where people in need are, I hope others will take on the long–term tasks required. We need to solve the problems of the mega–cities and mega–slums in those communities, or we will be solving them when significant numbers of mega–slum dwellers move to our cities.

# MEMORANDUM

To: The Commissioner of Planning
From: Allan Bonner
Date: January 1, 2092
Subject: Report on Toronto Neighbourhoods

This year will feature major celebrations of the 600th anniversary of European arrival in North America and what may be the 350th year in Toronto. First Nations have used Toronto as a meeting and trading place since time immemorial, so we have just picked an arbitrary date to take stock. Among other things, we are reflecting on how our city functions.

It's a shame the late mayor of Montreal, Jean Drapeau, didn't live to see the new gateway to North America. He thought it would be Mirabel Airport North of Montreal. Supersonic jets would land there. Travellers would then transfer to high speed rail to New York and other destinations. Well, it took a while and it took new technology, but his dream was essentially realized.

The new airport is in Lake Ontario and uses floating technology pioneered by the Japanese. The undulating motion of the floating structure generates electricity as do nearby floating windmills. Police boats patrol the perimeter at all times and there are also underwater cameras, remote sensing and scuba divers to ensure safety. With no neighbours, scramjets and all types of airplanes take off and land without complaint. With constructed airports in Hong Kong and Osaka dating to the last century, it's a wonder it took North America so long to relocate an airport in the water.

What's also a wonder is why North Americans didn't see the model right in front of their eyes. The Erie Canal was the model of new technology that lead to prosperity. Entrepreneurs began using barges to transport goods. They put on raw materials and finished products at communities along the way and others, in turn, put on their products and materials. One person's output became input for another's finished product or output. Grain became feed for animals, which became food for humans. Trees were the input for sawmills and the sawmills' output of lumber became the raw material with which carpenters built homes, barns and inns.

The Erie Canal was paid for before it was finished. People along the route made more money than they ever imagined. People made money in ways people had never made money before.

The same thing happened with the floating airport. New security provisions under, above and around the facility made this the preferred destination for tourists, business travelers and for freight. The ability to operate all hours of the day without disturbing neighbours allowed this airport to handle more traffic, more cost-effectively than any other airport in North America. The floating technology allowed operators to extend or add runways or change the angle and position of the entire airport to accommodate different volumes of traffic, seasonal weather conditions and destinations of travellers.

Fast connections to eastern seaboard and Great Lake cities made most local airports around Lake Ontario obsolete. Most were closed down and some were downsized to accommodate local, general aviation. This freed up large tracts of prime real estate, helping to finance the floating airport, floating causeways, high-speed rail, monorail and ferries. These connections offered several ways for freight and travelers to move on after landing at the airport. High-speed naturally costs more but passengers and freight customers make their decisions, in part with this in mind. Occasionally bad weather diverts travelers from ferries to trains or buses, but with multiple transport systems, there is always a way to get to the final destination.

Toronto's monorail began as a tourist curiosity. It connected several lakefront attractions – Ontario Place, The Canadian National Exhibition grounds and Centreville on Centre Island. It quickly became apparent that this novelty item was being used in an unintended way. Commuters were getting on the monorail at the western end of the CNE grounds at almost Dufferin and King and getting off on Centre Island and taking the existing ferry to downtown. The obvious next step was to create stops at all three islands, the island airport, downtown, and the Leslie Street Spit. This effectively linked up the recently densified condo corridor between Dufferin Street and Leslieville, including the Distillery District. It also linked major transport infrastructure at Union Station (trains, subways and buses) with multiple stops on these lines. One result was that if train service were interrupted, passengers could exit at the Exhibition station and transfer to the monorail or vice versa. The monorail also had stops on the major north–south bus and trolley–bus lines such as Broadview, Leslie, Spadina, Bathurst, and Dufferin.

As was the case with the Erie Canal, people were quick to see the social and economic benefits. It wasn't long until the monorail stretched out both east and west linking up with the east–west Bloor–Danforth subway line in a giant 'U' shape, planned many decades earlier.

The reference to trolley buses above should be clarified. Streetcars have long been replaced in Toronto. Once thought to be iconic, civic leaders did attitudinal studies to determine the self–evident – few people far away from Toronto knew of the street cars and fewer still considered them to be an icon worthy of drawing tourists or

*High Speed Rail, Domestic Eurostar in Paris.*
*European studies show that high–speed rail makes many air routes redundant, attracts automobile users and thus takes cars off the road. But they also attract new users – people who don't seem to use any form of transport. Build it and they will ride.*

convention goers. The icon was in the eye of the beholder – Torontonians. The dilemma was the icon's danger and inefficiency. Metal wheels on metal tracks make the vehicle hard to start up and stop, consume too much energy, and are more dangerous, especially for pedestrians. Rubber–tired vehicles are more efficient and safer.

The diversionary technique to wean Torontonians off their streetcars involved providing them with other icons. The monorail and cable car were the main substitutes. Some historic street cars still run on tourist–oriented routes, particularly Spadina station to Union Station and this takes passengers along the waterfront route on Queen's Quay. Promotional pictures of all three icons included airplanes taking off from the island airport, creating the effect of a school textbook on transport systems. With this celebrated use of the streetcars, Torontonians didn't protest when most other routes were converted to the safer and less costly buses. About every third bus is an electric trolley bus, used on these routes mainly to obtain full value from the existing overhead electrified lines.

The cable car of the kind we usually see on ski hills began as a feature of the Pan–American games in the Distillery District. The original plan was to transport visiting athletes and tourists from the site of the games to the pastoral Leslie Street Spit and Toronto Islands. The volume of ridership encouraged the extension of the line to include additional stops at the island airport and mainland locations.

This simple technology has spread to most major urban areas. Toronto uses them to traverse the Don Valley, for example. They are also in use to cross Burrard Inlet in Vancouver, the Bow River in Calgary, the North Saskatchewan in Edmonton, the Red and Assiniboine in Winnipeg, the Saint John in Fredericton and the harbour in Halifax. They are a natural way to take people up Mount Royal in Montreal as well – after all it's ski hill technology on a hill on which people used to ski.

The easiest and most cost–effective measure was the installation of distance markers showing residents and visitors how far they are from various attractions. This is done in Berlin and on the Skytrain route outside Vancouver. The tourist application involves promoting various attractions that might otherwise be missed. The application for local residents is to encourage them to walk more. Cities can be intimidating and even confusing, even for long–time residents. They get used to certain routes, using cars, taxis or transit. If they encounter a sign indicating that an interesting destination is a certain distance and walking time away, they are temped to walk. The distance that an individual is prepared to walk is a personal matter. People may choose increments anywhere from ten minutes to more than an hour, but markers do increase walking when people consider they may arrive a their destination more quickly than they could by cab, car or transit.

# Air Quality

Air currents don't respect civic, provincial or national boundaries. Toronto is occasionally downwind from urban and industrial pollution in Hamilton and America's Ohio Valley. However, the positive effects of US high–speed rail and monorail, nuclear power generation, electric cars (feeding surplus power back into the grid) and improved gas mileage have been felt in the neighbourhood.[1] These factors and Hamilton's steel works converting to the production of carbon fiber building materials means that this neighbourhood can see many positive effects at ground level.

Both Pearson and the island airports have been the source of concern over noise and air pollution for many years. Neighbourhood air is better quality as a result of less air traffic and fewer cars, taxis and buses taking travellers to the airports. High speed rail and monorail eliminated many short airline routes, as the TGV did in Europe. Integration of rail, monorail and airports replaces the old 'hub' system of airline travel, and reduces the necessity to change modes of travel or airplanes.[2] Now if people want to travel to most destinations between Chicago and Quebec City and south through America's megalopolis, they do so by rail for trips lasting fewer than five hours.[3] Air travel is reserved for small, remote locations or longer flights. One result is that there are fewer take–offs and landings at airports, but more passengers moved over a longer distance per flight.[4] The gondola to Toronto's island airport and the use of longer–haul, but quieter and more fuel efficient jets has made that facility popular. The redundant means of getting to the island airport is the old ferry as well as the tunnel begun in 1935 and finished about 80 years later.[5] Full life–cycle studies of the use of airport limos, taxis and the effects of flight delays have shown that the increased use of this facility has resulted in less air pollution and fewer highway traffic deaths.

There have always been strong arguments against 're-locating the problem' by generating power in coal–fired plants to run electric streetcars. However, Ontario's development of small, run–of–the–river generating plants created solutions in two locations rather than a problem in one. The test case was a GE run of the river plant built about 200 years ago and given to Trent University.[6] Even the old and inefficient turbines were generating about 70% of the power needed by 12,000 university students running computers, air conditioning and other appliances. Upgrading the existing turbines and adding one more produced about 120% of Trent's needs. This allowed the university to sell power back into the smart grid, power emergency services and be an evacuation centre in case of crisis. The area served by Trent can never be a victim of a general brown out. The neighbourhood is partially powered by hundreds of such run–of–the–river plants.

The floating causeway, airport, regional runways and urban amenities also generate some power through the undulating action of the water, captured by turbines affixed to the bottom of the floating technology. This initiative, alternative energy and conservation resulted in Ontario's traditional reliance on hydro and nuclear power remaining at 50% or more, despite increased demand.[7]

Neighbourhood residents appear to be excited about playing their part in maintaining a sustainable environment. A new generation of insulation caused power consumption to plummet. But still, many businesses and residents are using aesthetically pleasing solar generating panels and small wind turbines to power their buildings

and sell small surpluses back into the smart grid. Meters in schools, hospitals and cultural institutions show power generation and consumption by categories such as homes, time of day, institutions, neighbourhoods, and so on. Some residents enjoy the competitive aspect. Schools use the meters and comparisons with other schools as teaching tools. The carbon fiber building forms and monorail seem to have created a new, environmental mindset. Regardless of cause, the use of sustainable and renewable power is the vogue in the neighbourhood.[8]

The monorail and ferry system necessitated new streetscape guidelines. These serve functional, aesthetic and environmental purposes. Many buildings have been retrofitted with overhangs and awnings that keep rain and snow off pedestrians, but let light through. Newer awnings also contain solar panels for power generation. Awnings let sunlight in when heat is required and keep it out when the object is to save money on cooling. Deciduous trees serve a similar function.

Use of carbon fiber as building material allows for pre-fabricated, woven building modules such as floors, walls, ceilings and such to be delivered to a site much like pre–cast concrete slabs are. These light weight modules contain plumbing, wiring, information technology and heating elements and thus allow building owners to order several new stories, most of which are woven on a loom in a remote factory, with details constructed onsite, and installed virtually overnight. For some applications, 3D printing of

*Our Cities Ourselves – Buenos Aires, Argentina*
Creating an equitable future requires enabling everyone to live in a healthy community. This vision sees a polluted industrialized port being transformed with active transport paths, transit options, green space and quality building stock.

entire buildings is preferred, but both have simplified new construction and renovations. Nanomaterials on surfaces have eliminated graffiti as well as normal wear and tear.

As a result of woven buildings, construction, heating, and maintenance costs have plummeted. Borrowing from the award–winning codicil home, the new stories constructed from woven technology contained some transparent fiber which acted as a greenhouse for small vegetable gardens in the sky.[9] Other efficiencies included solar collectors woven into the building walls and roofs, optional air permeability for cooling in the summer and super–insulation for winter months.

Major intensification occurred as a result of the 'City in the Sky' program. A series of projects such as the elevated monorail, High Line trails, gondola and Toronto's version of +15 pedways means that these new and quickly built additional floors are easily linked. Other than for people with access challenges, there is little need for elevators in buildings that are up to six stories high. Monorails allow passengers to disembark at floors three or four and it has become fashionable to walk up two or down four flights of stairs, in part as a result of the 'Healthy City' initiative. Signs in buildings indicate that it takes a healthy person just one minute to walk down six flights of stairs – less than the time the average elevator takes. Other signs indicate that the walk up six flights of stairs is about 1.5 minutes for a healthy person.[10] If the elevator stops just once, walking is usually faster. Elevators and escalators are used mostly in emergencies and for those needing assistance. However, many neighbourhood residents find they might negotiate up or down no more than one or two levels during the course of a day and are a few stories above grade most of the time as they shop, work and socialize. Some are calling this the "three–sided street."[11]

The tall buildings near the subject lands that have been retrofitted with additional carbon fiber floors had an effect on the neighbourhood. The breathable woven fiber all but eliminates sway, making higher buildings possible– whether new or retrofitted. There is a nice synergy between the increased residential and retail density in the neighbourhood and the office jobs in the nearby fiber skyscrapers. Neighbourhood residents walk to work, encouraged by distance markers. It turns out that most fit people will walk for 20 minutes and are surprised at how far they can get. A few will walk for just under an hour. Distance

*Gate Tower Building, Osaka, Japan*
*A highway built through a highrise was a compromise between the government and the landowners. Would elevated infrastructure still be an eyesore if they were enclosed within buildings?*

127

**Carbon Fibre Lattice Tower**
*Strong and cost effective, carbon fibre is widely used to retrofit existing infrastructure and make new construction far more resilient. Lighter than steel, towers constructed of this material allow for additional savings in durability, construction time and resources required.*

The benefits of synergy are flowing two ways, just as pedestrian traffic does in the neighbourhood. Tens of thousands of people walk in all directions and flood the streets with people safely. Happily for the restaurants and bars nearby, many patrons support these establishments. There is a tolerance for increased density in and around the neighbourhood.[12] Regardless, office workers use local stores for snacks, dry cleaning and services such as hair cutting and shoe repair. Flower shops and high quality take–out restaurants do particularly well.[13]

Office workers don't all leave the buildings that surround the neighbourhood at the same time. Community residents don't all leave for work or arrive home at the same time. In part inspired by pandemic planning, telecommuting and flex hours have reduced the volume of people on the move during rush hour and extended the heaviest commuting times over about a four hour period at the beginning and end of the work day. This made redundancy more easily achievable. Office workers traverse the neighbourhood to get home, to the ferry system running between Oshawa and Oakville (and St. Catharines during the Shaw Festival), to monorail stations, to the gondola and so on. This keeps the neighbourhood lively about 15 hours per day.

markers indicate how long it takes to walk to certain major intersections and attractions. Full life–cycle analysis and benefits are hard to calculate since there have been other lifestyle changes, developments in drugs, medical treatment, and so on. However, there is no doubt that the countless people who walk are a little fitter, are not clogging the streets with cars, and may even be more alert and less stressed at home and work. Increased productivity could not be measured accurately and no current economic model can definitively link slightly lower cases of diabetes, heart disease and road rage to this phenomenon.

## General Environmental Matters

The neighbourhood benefits enormously from the by–law banning small engines of any kind. The banning of leaf blowers, lawn mowers, hedge clippers, weed whackers, and all such equipment immediately eliminated about 20% of air pollution and the noise associated with these devices. The slow growing grass developed at the University of Florida near the end of the 20th century made lawn mowers all but unnecessary.[14] Slow growing ivy is a popular ground cover. What does need snipping and clipping is done by relatively quiet, electric machines or by hand. The support for the ban may have resulted from increased environmental awareness, or a result of increased density. More people living, working, playing and learning more closely together may have become less tolerant of one resident using these noisy and noxious machines.

## Recreation

Towable and floating neighbourhoods trace their origin in Toronto to Buckminster Fuller.[15] Neighbourhood children aren't bused to camps north of the city anymore. Fresh air funds are used to adapt oil rig technology to create and maintain floating and towable neighbourhoods. Some are used as dormitories as far away as Queen's Univer-

**Bike The Floating Stadium**
*Nestled in the heart of downtown, this floating stadium makes use of the city's fixed transport network, local goods and services and density to host a local soccer match, floats down the river to host a concert, and returns by the weekend to be transformed into a public beach.*

sity in Kingston and at Brock University in St. Catharines during peak student needs. Others were docked near the West Don Lands to augment athlete housing for the Pan–Am Games. Some are used when an industrial need presents itself in Port Colborne or elsewhere, and the Shaw Festival has used them for housing actors and additional stages. The most relevant use for the neighbourhood is simply as a playground for families. One towable neighbourhood is docked near the subject neighbourhood's lake access point each May 24th weekend and families enjoy the open sky, fresh air, lake breezes and sunshine. These are now the neighbourhood's redundant parks, recreation facilities, cultural amenities and accommodation. The floating technology supports an area large enough for camping, small rental cottages, free day use, picnic and barbeque areas, and a variety of other uses, finally realizing Jane Jacobs' enthusiasm for building in the lake, which she called "the most important advance in planning for cities that has been made this century."[16]

The promotion of house boats is working better than predicted. The inexpensive and small structures, using Pullman technology, house families for weekends and holidays. The combination of public and private ownership and rental use mimics housing developments of decades before which featured market rent, low end of market rent, rent geared to income and other formulae. In both cases it is hard to determine who is paying what or owns what. Attractive houseboats line both the Don and Humber Rivers, are along the lake and around the islands and the Leslie

**Bike The Floating Stadium**
*Converted into a pool, the floating stadium makes a compelling venue for families to enjoy a relaxing summer's day at the water's edge.*

**Bike The Floating Stadium**
*Surrounded by walkable ramps at multiple levels, the floating stadium provides a multi–use pathway for cyclists and families out for a stroll at the water's edge.*

Street Spit.[17] These serve as getaways for neighbourhood residents who use them for a night, weekend, week or season, depending on need and ability to pay. These houseboats serve the same function as Muskoka cottages for more wealthy Torontonians, but have the advantage of short commutes. They are popular with people of all economic strata, and they level at least one playing field. Many more Torontonians can now say they are going 'to the cottage' – taking the prestige and mystery out of the phrase. The redundant transport system by which some neighbourhood residents go to traditional cottages on Georgian Bay, is the Georgian Bay ship canal first investi-gated in the 1840s and finished last year.[18]

Unions have played a positive role in the development of houseboats and floating neighbourhoods. In addition to building remote facilities on ski hills, at lakes and on farmland for the enjoyment of their members, several unions have underwritten the purchase and maintenance of houseboats and floating neighbourhoods. Union members receive a discount on rental, as do employer associations and pension funds which have underwritten some facilities. These amenities have become a factor in recruitment and retention and help keep Toronto well–stocked with talented workers.[19]

# Boundaries and Edges

Natural edges and boundaries always present opportunities and concerns.[20] Obvious ones include rivers, lakes, roads, railways and so on. Less obvious are the stairs leading to second and third story residential and retail. In addition to making upper floors inaccessible to those with mobility challenges, this boundary reduces rents, lessens appeal of the space and increases vacancies. The monorail and the City in the Sky program all but eliminated these boundaries. More ephemeral boundaries include levels of sunshine, noise, wind, views and other matters. These ephemeral boundaries must still exist in the neighbourhood, but are not obvious. This is mainly because of the solar powered 'smart awnings' which adjust to sun, wind, temperature and precipitation. Both vertical and horizontal, they shield pedestrians from the elements and direct fresh air onto city streets. Some refer to these carbon fibre awnings as the lungs of the city.

Toronto's waterways – the Humber, Don and lakefront – have become porous. The boundary has been breached both physically and psychologically as a result of a number of factors. The houseboat program has reminded Torontonians

that they live between two rivers and on a lake. The waterways have become places to live, work, play and learn. A result is cleaner waterways because all residents have become aware that what goes down the waste pipe eventually comes back to the drinking fountain. The transport systems that use and traverse the waterways have also reduced the edge or boundary effect. Neighbourhood residents occasionally use the gondola or monorail and ride above the Don and Humber. They walk to a ferry dock where the neighbourhood meets Lake Ontario and take the ferry system east and west. Entering or traversing a waterway feels natural and seamless. The waterways are extensions of the neighbourhood, harkening back to Canada's beginnings when they were our transport system. The perspectives that citizens get from the air on the monorail and gondola help them gain their bearings in their city, increasing "imageability."[21]

The elevated Gardiner Expressway, long a major psychological and physical boundary, has also become an extension of the neighbourhood. There are restaurants underneath the structure, much like the ones in London (Bridges Restaurant) and New York (Grand Central Station and High Line Park).[22] As in Vancouver, there are also offices, bike rentals, storage lockers, residents and other uses that bring community members to the area, rather than repel them. Portions of the Gardiner have been torn down, but what remains is well used as a community resource.

Beside the pillars of the Gardner, and fifteen or so feet in the air, the cantilevered jogging tracks, bicycle tracks, plantings, walkways, small coffee shops, and restaurants attract people for a variety of uses.[23] This has caused some to quip that had the structure not existed, the Parks Commissioner might have built it and nearby residents might have lobbied for it. The carbon fibre overhanging structure also serves to shed the rain and light snow, creating another pedestrian walkway.

On the roadway of the Gardiner, the 'neglect the roads' program has worked well.[24] One full lane remains closed to accommodate the one foot in diameter carbon fiber monorail support pylons. The remaining portion of the lane is landscaped and used as a park, assessable via monorail stops and arched fibre pedways diagonally traversing the remaining traffic lanes. Neighbourhood residents enjoy much of their city from multiple heights along the Gardiner, and in multiple ways – on foot, bicycle, jogging, by car, and by monorail. From the ground to above the monorail, there are up to six different levels in some locations. Direct access to the hotels, condos and office buildings either side of the Gardiner has created a new neighbourhood between floors three and six, accessible via monorail stops and by foot. One can walk from Liberty Village at roughly Dufferin, to Distillery at about the Don River without touching the ground. The gondola also connects these two spots via the islands and the Leslie Street Spit. Much of the route can be taken under a canopy of carbon fiber and thus used comfortably even during light snow or rain. Movable and computer controlled, aesthetically pleasing carbon fibre baffles block much of the wind during less favourable weather and are used at all levels on the Gardiner as they are at several locations in the neighbourhood.

The elevated expressway has ceased to be a boundary in another way. People movers made of carbon fibre moving sidewalks take those with mobility challenges on gentle grades to the four different levels. Sticky surfaces grip walkers, wheelchairs, scooters and other devices to make the short trip safe and easy. There are seats for those who need them. People movers are powered by solar collectors woven in to the carbon fibre. Heating the public washrooms is achieved with passive solar with liquid circulation through tubes in the woven structure, augmented[25] by geothermal brine.[26] Woven circuits (first used in the 1960s) make all systems 'smart' and control the driverless

*The High Line, New York City*
*Created from a converted abandoned elevated railway bed, this unique urban park in New York has revitalized the public realm below and above the walkway, raised property values, and added additional green space to the city.*

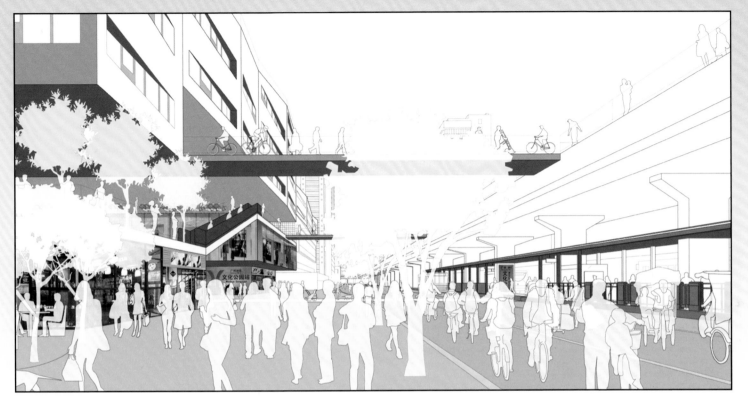

**Our Cities Ourselves –
Guangzhou, China**
*As our aged highways are
increasingly unable to
support the weight of traffic,
must we really choose
between demolition and
extensive repair? This vision
sees an elevated highway
being repurposed as an
active transport route with
shops and building
entrances, invigorating not
only the street level, but the
elevated public realm above.*

monorail, regulate the traffic flow, provide security, and run the people movers. Traffic volume on the Gardner and the Lake Shore below is being held steady because of drivers switching to the ferry system, monorail, vintage street cars and gondola.

Vintage street cars appeal to tourists.[27] Riders on the vintage cars pay double the fare to ride between Spadina and Union stations. Selected other routes, including one through the neighbourhood, are popular among groups who want to rent a car for tours or parties. Those who don't want to pay extra wait for the next car since only every third car is vintage.

In the neighbourhood, some level crossings now feature car and pedestrian traffic flowing unimpeded above or below a sunken or elevated track. Some roadways and walkways blend seamlessly into gradually slopped carbon fibre ramps that take both people and vehicles over tracks with many not noticing the barrier beneath. Some railway tracks have been dwarfed by the monorails and Skytrain using their rights of way above the railbed.[28]

135

However, some heavy rail still exists. Luckily, renewed interest in rail travel, including in the monorail, Skytrains, LRTs and heavy rail seems to have brought back some of the romance and wonder. What heavy rail remains is thus less of a psychological barrier. On a more banal level, use of the linear induction engine, rubber not steel wheels where possible, and alternative energy has made all rail cleaner, most quieter, and some virtually silent.[29] The barrier of the acoustic footprint of rail is thus less. Also there are simply fewer heavy rail trains traversing the neighbourhood as a result of the monorail running above the tracks, and the ferry system and causeway running along the lake. Rubber tired trolley buses are safer, quieter and a little more mobile in traffic.[30]

Translucent and some transparent carbon fibre walls provide an unobtrusive but stronger safety barrier between

*Our Cities Ourselves –*
*Ahmedabad, India*
*When an area is unsafe for pedestrians because of vehicular traffic, people are inhibited from interacting. This vision sees an area suffering from the dominance of motorcycles, cars and motorized rickshaws redeveloped into a pedestrian focused area with mixed use buildings and waterfront connections.*

such hazards as roads and railway tracks and the neighbourhood. Parents are a little less concerned for their children's safety as a result. There is the added benefit of the 'smart' walls also providing a solar powered community notice board. Viewers need cheap glasses to view notices, so for those who consider the signage visual pollution, the viewing is optional. Emergency announcements can be seen without the glasses. Signage is also a vehicle to raise money for community events and charities.[31]

These smart walls have a medical use as well. Pedestrians can use their inexpensive glasses to access the web. The smart wall can read palm prints and scan retinas. The user can obtain a range of medical data in real time and even rudimentary suggestions on diet and lifestyle improvements. In emergencies the user is directed to the appropriate health care professional.

**Our Cities Ourselves – New York City, USA**
*One of the most pleasant experiences in New York is walking across the Brooklyn Bridge. Instead of tearing down the elevated expressways in some of our cities, we could create a walking or biking path after installing rapid transit above or below. Our aging infrastructure, such as bridges that can't withstand heavy traffic anymore, could be repurposed as urban walking parks.*

# Cultural Implications

The area below the monorail forms a pleasant enclave, much like the one at the Gardiner at grade level, but with little or no auto traffic. There are some permanent uses in this area, similar to the ones under the Gardiner. But the ad hoc uses may be of most interest. On the anniversary of the Tiananmen Square protest, the Chinese community reproduced 'Democracy Wall,' using holograms and other images projected by technology imbedded in the carbon fiber. Germans celebrated the anniversary of the fall of the Berlin Wall with a display of images sent over from the Wall Museum in Berlin. On Remembrance Day, images of World War I trenches, Vimy Ridge and notable Canadian battles from all wars are projected on and by the fiber walls.[32] The labour movement regularly commemorates the Regina riot, Winnipeg general strike and historic gains in occupational health and safety. On many occasions a specially equipped monorail car is put on a siding and the neighbourhood benefits from travelling exhibits.

Even when there isn't a special or commemorative event, the area is still special. On most weekends it has the vibrant feel of London's Portobello Road, Sydney's King's Cross, the Paris flea market, Vancouver's Granville Island or Hong Kong's Stanley Market. There is a seasonal farmers' market with much produce coming down on the monorail from Holland Marsh, on a line that goes up the 400 Highway and also serves Barrie, Collingwood, and points north. There are entrepreneurs providing hair cuts and the obligatory knife sharpener seems to be the same older gentleman who has been ringing a bell in residential areas for a hundred and fifty years. Swap meets at which residents trade unwanted household items cut down on waste. A casual stroller can buy a variety of food from a dozen cultures from licensed vendors, get shoes repaired, minor mending, hear live music, and obtain a tarot card reading.

The redundant transport systems both in and out of the neighbourhood have made some free transit and toll roads and highways (FAT) possible.[33] Because residents have a choice, they have accepted additional toll roads on the 407 model, but adding the Finance Maintain elements to DBFM (Design, Build, Finance, Maintain) with ownership remaining in public hands. This revenue has in part subsidized some parallel and free transit systems. Personal transponders make paying fares automatic and makes transfers among modes seamless (taxi, TTC, intercity monorail, air), with fairly seamless baggage handling as well.

## Social Services

The neighbourhood has long had a problem with homelessness and the provision of social services. Building on the tradition of mobile services such as meals on wheels, the Victorian Order of Nurses (VON), mobile libraries, flying doctors in Australia and flying legal services in Canada, the monorail brought a wealth of services to the neighbourhood. It began with such provincial agencies as Royal Ontario Museum, the Art Gallery of Ontario, The Ontario Science Centre, Science North, The McMichael Canadian Collection and TVOntario.[34] Then, the London Children's Museum, The Algonquins of Golden Lake, the water and environmental experts at Trent University, and Ottawa's museums and galleries participated. They and their ministerial sponsors funded the projects. Each spring, these and other institutions hold job fairs, including help with resume writing and interviewing skills for students looking for work. They are assisted by various ministries including Education, Economic Development, Colleges and Universities and others, in partnership with some industry sponsors.

Social services are now more available. Specially equipped monorail cars regularly dock on sidings in school yards and other locations. Residents can obtain flu shots, see a chiropodist and get cuts and bruises tended to. Without drawing attention to the service, the car also houses a psychiatrist and psychologist to tend to both the homeless and other residents who might need these services. Some cars are labelled to attract families and are staffed by family practice specialists. Teenagers and abused spouses can obtain help without publicity or stigma. Practitioners refer clients to other monorail stops for privacy or safety. Multiple monorail stops of this kind spread the treatment and thus the clients more broadly through the city, reducing the tendency to ghettoize the people or the treatment.[35]

Some monorail cars are specially equipped and staffed by institutions with special expertise. Baycrest Hospital lends its geriatric expertise. Sunnybrook Hospital has a car for veterans' services, and the Canadian Association for Mental Health (CAMH) tends to substance abusers and those with mental challenges. Women's College Hospital lends its family practice expertise.

*Sydney monorail, Chinatown*
*The Sydney monorail only went around in a circle, regrettably, but it did enliven upper floors of real estate.*

# Funding

Funding is a fundamental aspect of sustainability.[36] Countless railways, airplane manufacturers, auto companies and airlines have failed – many in Canada. In order to keep the quality of life maintained in the neighbourhood, the transport and infrastructure programs surrounding the neighbourhood have to be sustainable. So do the manifestations of those programs within the neighbourhood. This study finds that creative initial funding and imaginative revenue streams appear to be sustainable.[37] This echoes the complex methodology and multiple funding sources used by Robert Moses to build the west side improvements and the many sources needed to make high–speed rail viable in California.[38] Multiple sources appear to be as important as harnessing both public and private funds and all levels of government.[39]

Advertising is a small revenue stream with signage on pillars, walls and in monorail stations. European experience has shown that ridership goes up on TGV systems more than ridership goes down on highways and in planes. So, revenue from new travellers helps as well. The system is underwritten in part by large buildings, hotels and the Toronto (CN) Tower that paid to have stations at their facility. Sports teams do the same, which has allowed fans to rent a monorail car and have it parked within view of several of our outdoor soccer and baseball fields. Families can also rent monorail cars equipped with Pullman technology and park them on the waterfront in cottage country, or on the causeway adjacent to one of the communities on Lake Ontario. These 'cottages' serve as another revenue stream.[42]

Full life cycle cost–benefit analysis shows the benefit to employers in having a more liveable work environment, less commuting, less lost time and a healthier population. Some funds from workers' compensation, the Ministries of Health and Labour, general revenue, and employer health taxes also support the systems.[43] Some galleries and museums from far outside the jurisdiction want the publicity that their 'wrapped' car and exhibit generates. The Getty, the Guggenheim, the Louvre, the Victoria and Albert (V&A) and the Museum of Modern Art (MOMA) are taking the lead.

A large source of funding for the monorail is from its multiple uses.[44] The average monorail in non–rush hour times, including overnight, might be carrying one passenger car and several cars for freight.[45] Usually one or two cars contain household and business waste destined for a large sorting and recycling depot half way to the hard rock landfill site where all that cannot be reused, composted, or recycled is deposited. The ash from burning for power generation goes to this same hard rock site. The emptied monorail cars return to the neighbourhood with aggregate, wood and stone for construction and renovation, produce from farms, and other cargo that would normally be trucked in. Carbon fiber and 3D printing make the need for these traditional building materials minimal.

Refrigerated cars move perishable goods. A removable

plastic bladder lines the cars to control odour. The bladder also allows the shipping of high flash point home heating fuel, bulk milk and other liquid products that would normally be moved on trucks. The fact that the monorail is almost impossible to derail and can take sharper turns and rapid variations in height makes this method of transport, even with passengers on the same train, much safer than trucking.

So, from Windsor to Quebec City, and through the neighbourhood, dozens of different revenue sources fund the system. In each major urban area a few stops within the city are funded by local passengers and there is a cost–saving achieved by cancelling some local bus routes. Longer distance commuters such as students and business people help fund the stops outside these urban areas. Tourists and mid– to long–distance occasional business travellers do their part too. Farmers, aggregate producers, lumber companies and refineries in Sarnia all usually have a car on the line. The federal government helps fund the movement of petroleum products as a redundant alternative to the TransCanada pipeline. Quebec cheese and Maritime fish and produce fill cars on the return trip to Ontario. Small manufacturers pool resources to rent space on monorail cars, in the same way they used to pay for space for a pallet on a truck using the highway or in a freight car on a train. Smaller vehicles move these goods from the monorail siding to their final destination.

One large revenue source was federal and provincial

**Food Delivery Cargo Bike**
*My mother used to call the local corner store and get provisions brought over in the carrier of a bike. We have new technology to keep staples cold, hot and safe in transit. Smart phones could summon freelance couriers to and from both the grocery store and customer.*

ministries responsible for security and emergency response. Since the redundant transport systems and other initiatives such as telecommuting have both a current and a future potential economic benefit, they are funded by the appropriate ministries. The prediction in the case of California's HSR that "the public sector may need to significantly mitigate the risk before the private sector will invest" has turned out to be true.[46]

Another revenue stream, using similar logic, comes from the insurance industry. Since about 50,000 North Americans die each year in car accidents, insurance companies are paying out benefits to survivors, and to the injured who hold policies. If injuries and deaths are fewer, payouts less, then the insurance companies get to keep more of the premiums for a longer period of time, or forever. These premiums are invested and making money for the insurance companies, so those contributing to this increased wealth should have a share. Off–loading risk may be of the greatest benefit to the primary insurer, so they, along with governments and citizen groups, have lobbied offshore reinsurance and retrocession companies. These offshore companies, learning of the reduced speed limits on roads and redundant mass transit systems in Canada, found this to be the most attractive and least risky jurisdiction from which to take a transfer of some risk. The government's role was to pass legislation increasing mandatory deductibles, sharing some of the risk, and producing another revenue stream.[47]

## Neglect the Roads Policy

The policy of diverting public funds from one hundred years of public subsidy of the automobile and trucking industries has worked well.[48] The volume of people moved by monorails and Skytrains compensated for the reduction in lanes on some portions of the Gardiner, DVP, QEW and portions of the 400 series of highways. Monorail and Skytrain stations allowed the construction of more density along these multi–modal corridors. Even in locations where pylons for the elevated transit did not close a lane, the oversized scale of some roads was aesthetically improved by the construction of elevated transit. In some urban locations a lane was closed for other uses (walking, cycling, landscaping). This produced a more human scale as the boulevard and lampposts do on Toronto's Palmerston Avenue, or as the boulevard tree plantings on 153rd Avenue and other wide streets in the north end of Edmonton have done. The elevated transit construction allowed for elevated walkways so that pedestrians can easily cross the Lake Shore, Gardiner and other wide roadways.

Diverting freight from trucks has saved a great deal of wear and tear on the roads.[49] So, while maintenance was technically neglected, it was not as necessary after a reduction in the volume of trucking. Enforcement of weight restrictions, load balancing, tire inflation and other measures reduced road maintenance as well. Taxing trucks to reflect the actual value of their use of roads and legislation requiring air suspension provided both revenue and reduced damage to roads. The tax on radial tires transferred risk from all taxpayers and citizens to those who buy and use these tires which damage roads a little more than nylon tires do.[50]

Speed limits were reduced on arterial roads and the 400 series to 90 kph. Exceptions include some lanes where cars with transponders can pay an additional fee to drive a little faster on a better maintained lane. A result was a huge saving in fuel and less loss of life in traffic accidents. Travellers wanting to go faster take higher speed rail. Residential streets in the neighbourhood now feature traffic calming measures that really work, including reduced speed limits.[51] Fewer neighbourhood residents use cars than ever before. Commute times are shorter because of measures which have eased congestion.

The driverless car has not caught on quite as well as predicted. Some expected a reduction in traffic by two–thirds when taxis, limos and shared vehicles took to the streets 24/7 without drivers, only needing to stop for repairs. Continuously driven cars don't need parking spaces – by definition. Moreover, car elevators allow a quadrupling of our available parking spaces. While driverless cars have made a huge positive impact, what no one predicted was the love of vintage cars and the number that are still on the road – much like previous generations' love of horses for pleasure riding long after they ceased to be a mode of transport.

## Density Sales and Transfers

Density transfers and the sale of density rights have long been a feature of the development, redevelopment and infill of mature cities. Under planning, community and political oversight, the neighbourhood has retained its religious and cultural institutions and obtained residential, commercial, retail or other uses on lands both within and outside its boundaries.

The TTC was the first public entity to benefit from density transfers.[52] Taking the example of decades old attempts by the MTA in New York to sell the density rights of subway tunnels under the Hudson River, the TTC developed a revenue stream by selling its density rights following environmental assessments and community consultations. Then it became apparent that if the TTC were involved in the property management of residential, retail and office condos, it could have a revenue stream in perpetuity. The property management company that was formed also managed the building on the former planetarium site and the new TVOntario (TVO) signature building, containing residential, retail and office space. Some residential units were designated for students of journalism and their professors, to facilitate practicums. While TVO didn't have density rights to sell, its status as an anchor and signature tenant–developer gave it leverage. So did the favourable conditions under which cultural industries could access public lands, co–locate on university land, receive and sell density rights as tax deductible gifts and so on. A similar mixed–use development on the grounds of the Ontario Science Centre houses student interns engaged in practicums, university professors and a satellite campus of the University of Ontario Institute of Technology. There are now secure revenue streams for these cultural institutions.[53]

There are several manifestations of this mixed–use,

intensification and co–location in the neighbourhood. First, purposeless open space is rare. The few apartment buildings in the neighbourhood which have set backs and 'park–like settings' have been filled in with a variety of uses that serve citizens at least eighteen hours a day. Parking lots are almost non–existent. Reliance on transit, walking and cycling has reduced the need. Some parking is underground and many cars are stacked in multiple vehicle units on the surface and below. Some of the surplus space has been used for urban parks with New York's Paley Park as the template. These small spaces, many under the monorail, contain waterfalls, fountains, and landscaping. They're a place for residents to sit and enjoy a beverage

from the nearby vendors' carts, along the lines of what was done under the overpasses where King meets Queen in the West Don Lands. When not in use, carts are stored in locked facilities under overpasses.[54]

Co–location for mixed use was driven by the public sector at first. Residents saw the benefit of having services, retail, educational and cultural uses near them. Schools now contain residential units for the caretaker, some teachers, and student teachers on practicums.[55] This parallels the high rise vertical schools in the UK which feature one grade per floor.[56] Some low end of market rent and rent geared to income units are used by visual and performing artists who also assist teachers. These units are sometimes

*Our Cities Ourselves –*
*Jakarta, Indonesia*
Sustainable transit hubs
combined smoothly with
retail and housing will be
vital to ensuring we can
accommodate population
growth while still ensuring a
comfortable quality of life.
This vision sees existing
communities being preserved
and enhanced though a
network of covered routes
and pedestrian pathways
surrounded by nature.

built above small police, health and ambulance stations and co–located at schools. These facilities also provide practicum opportunities for students and enrichment opportunities for teachers. The school library is open to the public after school and on weekends. Athletic facilities have become community facilities, staffed in part by physical education students on practicums; part of a national public service program. Public support for these amenities morphed into public support for schools transferring their density rights to other users. The student and caretaker housing was seen as a means to make amenities available to the community and keep them tidy – generating public support.

But the most creative and beneficial aspect of density transfers pertained to the development of the monorail. The monorail's first revenue generation occurred long before it was built. Awarded density rights for its stations and track, the authority constructing and running the monorail began using this repository of value to foster mixed use development at its stations, sometimes in conjunction with the building owners adjacent to stops.[57] Along the route, density was sold to the owners of low–rise buildings on the route so they could develop several additional floors or entire new sites. If building owners couldn't afford to buy density rights, they were encouraged to form a condominium corporation to share risk and reward. In some cases, density rights were sold to projects many blocks away from the monorail route for positive social purposes. Transactions were vetted by communities, and in the planning and political process.[58]

## Proposal Calls

Remarkably, the public sector probably played a larger role than the private sector in the many changes one can see in the neighbourhood. Using public sector spending power (40% of GDP), legislation, regulations and enforcement seems to have had more effect than the development fees and taxes paid by the private sector. It is hard to quantify the enormous benefit of the visible use of cultural agencies and public institutions (police, fire, ambulance, education, social services, emergency measures) in setting a tone and an example of future development, but it must have been an influential factor–much like the police station in the Distillery District.[59]

I should also mention the benefits of world–wide proposal calls. While many received scant response, and some which did receive multiple responses did not proceed, a few were very successful. Open ended RFPs were issued with specifications for a structure, service or public amenity. Bidders were free to submit a 'cost plus' bid, or one that recaptured cost and profit from users. Bidders were required to submit a formula for calculating user fees and a date on which the city would have ownership of the amenity, if ever. This resulted in some monorail stations and ferry terminals (containing hotels, restaurants and other amenities) being built quickly. The gondola was entirely privately built and this was deemed acceptable by the public because it is mainly for tourist and island airport users, with residents of the island being able to use the existing ferries and tunnel.[60] One enterprising company repatriated antique TTC street cars from Cairo and ran them during tourist season, paying the TTC for the right to do so, in the same way that VIA rail rents track from the railways. The fact that users have a public option seems to have made this private sector involvement acceptable.

## Condominiums in the Sky

The Condominium Act has long anticipated the residents of different buildings forming a corporation and managing amenities in a third structure. This has not been a normal use of the provisions of the Act until the last few years after some revisions. The manifestations are many in the neighbourhood. Along the monorail route, enterprising business and residential owners have formed condominium corporations for several purposes. Fees are funding litter pick up, extra police officers, private security, maintenance, landscaping, recreation facilities, urban parks, social services, and even shuttle buses. Reserve funds are set aside for major repairs and upgrades. Once this unusual method caught on, these corporations became as prevalent and 'normal' as business improvement districts.[61]

# Conclusion

What was the rationale for the redundant transport systems? Looking back, it's hard to determine which argument was most persuasive. Environmentalists noted that mass transit was one of the most effective ways to combat air pollution. Civic boosters wanted a tourist attraction and symbols of modernity. Some property owners wanted the increased value that transit access generates. Community groups were lobbying for transit to ease the commuting time. No doubt some private developers, small building owners and those answering proposal calls only wanted profits. Cultural industries funded by the government wanted to demonstrate 'interagency cooperation.' Emergency responders are always keen to experiment with new 'kit.'

Expected outcomes also contain surprises. No one predicted that the area beneath the monorail would become as attractive to community members as it has. It appears people want a reason and a place to congregate. Residents and visitors alike seem to enjoy vibrant street life as a pleasant unexpected outcome of the construction of the redundant transport system. The transport system, carbon fiber and the increased density that both permitted created an unexpected synergy. No one predicted the success of co–location of mixed use on both private and public lands.

The implications for the planning process in Toronto are clearer than historical causes and effects. It seems clear that all levels of government have a role to play. That role may be passive in merely allowing a measure to proceed without attempts to block it. That role may also include a range of active involvement from the passing of bylaws through to the funding and encouragement of the co–location of public services on a site.

*Our Cities Ourselves –*
*Buenos Aires, Argentina*
*Around the world, deindustrialization has blighted streetscapes, leaving communities with abandoned buildings and bereft of quality jobs. Reclaiming and redeveloping distressed sites within our urban regions is becoming commonplace. Will the outcome help create an equitable world?*

*Our Cities Ourselves –*
*Jakarta, Indonesia*
*New building materials may help us take a great leap forward. Carbon fibre has many times the strength of steal and a fraction of the weight. It's at least possible to fabricate building walls on an industrial look that could make tall buildings resistant to sway, since the carbon fibre is air permeable. How many unique sustainable building approaches can you see being used here?*

The benefit of citizen support for a planning measure is also clear. People are legitimately self–interested. Their first concern is themselves, their families, neighbours and neighbourhood. Showing citizens 'what's in it for them' can break a log jam of generic resistance and change a neighbourhood.[62] Once a person, her circle of friends, and neighbourhood are looked after, it appears that this person may then be ready to take action to improve conditions in the wider community and matters farther afield. So, public consultations in a respectful atmosphere of as much full disclosure of options and outcomes as possible, is key.

New technology is also key. Plans and planning policy depend on the art of the possible. New building materials and techniques can spark building forms and social organization that is disruptive and fundamentally life changing.

What is also clear is the need for further and vigorous

research. It's important to study monorails further, within the commitment to some form of urban and interurban high–speed rail (HSR), including the elevated kind. Density transfers must be managed closely and protocols must be established for how far away from a site is too far to transfer. The roles of the public and private sector can be controversial, as can proposal calls and design, build, finance and maintain (DBFM). There will be a debate about what is pleasant integration versus overpowering superimposition, and whether to superimpose or begin again on an open site such as Lake Ontario. Whether systems are parallel, integrated at grade, below or above will also be an interesting question to continue exploring. Finally, the most vexing is probably public consultations and support. Ways and means to achieve acquiescence, let alone support, need much study.

In the end, we're back to the notion that everything is connected to everything else. Modern planners need to have 360 degree vision with eyes on the political process at all levels of government, creative funding techniques, partnerships, legitimate self–interests, community wants and fears and a host of other issues. It may not be possible to make all cities or neighbourhoods as liveable as the one studied in this report, but without that 360 degree vision, it will be surely much harder, if not impossible.

# Epilogue

This research and writing project had simple beginnings. I was shocked at news coverage of the handling of the New Orleans evacuation, and subsequent evacuation of Houston after Hurricane Katrina. I was also shocked at the inadequacy of my city's emergency plan. This motivated me to research urban evacuation and safety during my studies to qualify for an MSc in planning. I was building on my work in risk, crisis and disaster management in my practice, also the subject of my studies at Leicester University in the UK.

Now, as this project is ending, I am shocked by a series of news stories: urban riots in several cities; flooding in Houston; forty tornados one night that threatened 30 million people; a tropical storm that hit the eastern seaboard; a fire that threatened a nuclear plant north of New York; a man who died while taking a safety course in Nova Scotia; and hundreds of millions of dollars spent on airport security that isn't effective.

During my research in urban emergency planning, I began doing radio and TV interviews on the topic. I also wrote newspaper and journal articles. After we had a power failure in my city of Toronto, The Toronto Star quoted me as asking the rhetorical question, "Who is the genius who decided to use social media (which needs power) to notify people that there is a power failure?" I received a call a day or two later while sitting in the green room of Canada AM, the national morning news program. The voice on the other end said "I'm that genius."

This call began an exchange of a dozen emails. Like many senior people, the caller was easily angered at criticism. Like many busy people in a complex organization, he didn't know the details of what was going on in his department. In this case, he didn't know what other means, if any, were available, to notify citizens that their power was off.

My research into 100 emergency plans for cities in Asia, North America and the UK taught me many things. Social media has promise, as you read in the main text of this book. But the battery life of hand-held devices is less than the duration of many power outages in Canada. Many cities acknowledge the potential futility of using devices which need power to warn people that there's no power. Many cities use alternatives – loudspeakers in helicopters, LED read-outs on power company vans, door-to-door visits, political-style lawn signs, doorknob hangers, sirens and other means. Houston is experimenting with "AlertFM" which can activate a strobe light or bed-shaker for people with special needs.

Then there was the New York organization dedicated to helping people who are victims of disasters. I was introduced by a mutual friend who thought I could help. In my first meeting the head of the group told me that she held training seminars and one of her protocols was to keep official emergency responders away from untrained volunteers. This was to prevent the volunteers from hampering the professionals. I provided this person with studies analyzing the value (and potential liability) that volunteers provide. In some emergencies, many of the official responders are dead or injured. Volunteers on the scene are defacto responders whether we like it or not. Best to train them up. In fact, the plan in Memphis notes that in Mexico City earthquakes, volunteers saved 800 people, but 100 volunteers died in the process. Memphis advocates training.

In fact, most of the 100 plans we reviewed have reference to harnessing and training volunteers. Many volunteers are provided with ID, safety gear, regular training, and specific jobs. Portland, Oregon, may be a leader in this area. Vancouver's Volunteer Corps (VVC) sets a good example. FEMA mandates such training. Homeland Security's Citizen Corps helps with training.

After some final research just before publication of this book, I became more adamant about improving emergency planning. In the spring of 2015, just before publication, Ashley McIntosh logged on to every site for a final time to determine if the city plans had been updated. She found that about 25% had been. That's not enough, and too many had only minor changes. She also found that we'd missed some things on our first pass. I wasn't surprised because one of our major findings was plans that weren't printer-friendly, had navigation problems, 401 errors, references to appendices that didn't exist, countless links, small font, unreadable maps, and so on. If we missed something, I bet a citizen or organization trying to plan for an emergency would miss something too.

We found both highlights and lowlights in this second review of emergency plans and this epilogue will share some of them. But, a cautionary tale – these lessons are frozen in time, bound to be updated with the next plan revision or technological advancement. As they say in legacy media – "Today's news is tomorrow's fish wrap." Today, it might be that today's Tweet lasts until the next Instagram. Plans may stagnate, improve, or get worse, the week after this book is published.

With that disclaimer, here's what we found.

## Some Good News

Some at the municipal level are dealing with climate change head on. There's no debate, and no euphemisms. Boston sets a great example. Climate change will cause small and large challenges. Even the small ones will cascade into bigger ones. Boston has recognized that more heat days means more danger for vulnerable people. Hundreds of Americans die each year from excessive heat. More die in Florida from the heat than from tornados and hurricanes combined. Heat will cause an even more sedentary lifestyle and a need to adjust work schedules. A quadrupling of poor air quality days will be trouble for people with respiratory problems. Boston has a lot of work to do with many roads, facilities, and even emergency centers in the flood plain, and which need repairs. A combination of shoreline erosion and rising sea-levels (8-16 inches) will cause real challenges on Boston's waterfront. Boston's plan notes that "by 2099, Massachusetts could have a climate similar to Maryland's" or the Carolinas.

Boston is taking action. They're not just talking and planning; they're doing. Their task force report on climate change is a wake-up call to do more with vegetation, architecture and response techniques. They've designed a park that also mitigates coastal flooding.

Boston has looked beyond our planet to spot danger. Plan writers note that sunspots can damage electrical grids and GPS. Three hundred large transformers in the US are vulnerable. A geomagnetic storm could cut power to 130 million people.

Some cities are good at providing advice on personal preparedness.

- Richmond, British Columbia, includes a link to a provincial emergency workbook with advice on water purification, hygiene, and keeping homes safer.

- Richmond also leads in designating disaster response routes which aren't for evacuation, but for moving response vehicles through an emergency to help citizens.

- Oakville, Ontario, lists the shelf life of stored food for sheltering in place.

- Mississauga, Ontario, has a summer emergency camp for teenagers.

- Oshawa, Ontario, has great information on hidden water sources in our homes, including in ice cube trays, hot water tanks, the toilet reserve tanks, and elsewhere.

- Philadelphia notes the value of spray paint in a home emergency kit – good for making large signs calling for help.

- Memphis advocates using construction methods resistant to mould and flooding.

- Guelph, Ontario, has good advice on car kit and go bag contents.

- New Orleans recognizes the dual loyalty of responders and runs safety seminars for their families, so responders won't be as tempted to look after loved ones and not show up to work.

But the emergency response community has not decided whether citizens should be able to shelter self-sufficiently for 36 hours, 72 hours or 7 days. Nor have responders decided whether a person needs two quarts, one gallon, two gallons, or three gallons of water per day to survive. Different plans advise different amounts.

## Some Bad News

However, these encouraging signs are far outweighed by weaknesses in most emergency plans. This is frustrating, because the few creative, specific and helpful plans show that cities can show citizens and organizations how to be safer. In fact, all they have to do is read each others' plans and copy the best.

The hubris of Syracuse to indicate it is the safest city in America is not a reason to have no plan. Fear of terrorism is no excuse for having secret plans for responders and web-based eye-candy for a vulnerable public.

The age of plans is still shocking. This is more so because the Emergency Management and Civil Protection Act in Ontario requires that municipalities have plans, hold simulations, and distribute amendments every year. Most jurisdictions have similar legislation.

Small examples may show how quickly plans go out of date. Many plans still refer to fax machines, which are fast disappearing. Others reference a "windshield survey" of damage, achieve by driving through hard hit areas – if they're drivable. Other plans speak of doing this kind of survey from an airplane, which one hopes is available at a serviceable airport, and accessible via passable roads – faint hopes. The aerial and windshield surveys have been outdated ever since drones were invented. There's no time in an emergency to battle through streets clogged with debris to get to an airport. If wedding photographers and pranksters are using drones, emergency responders should as well. These drones can not only survey damage, but also find injured and trapped citizens.

Geography and history are often ignored in emergency plans. Toronto, Ontario, site of Hurricane Hazel (1954) which devastated the city, has three dams, 2400 susceptible structures and 14,000 people who live and/or work in the flood plain. The same is true in Boston, Philadelphia, and many other cities that have vital assets on the flood plain, including emergency response facilities. Many emergency facilities need repair or strengthening, as well.

In many plans I see the illusion of 'expanded time.' This is a concept that allows emergency managers to talk through tasks or issues in a table top simulation and come to the conclusion that they are prepared and could handle an event. But they forget that saying that "Bob will mobilize school buses" takes less than a second to say, but may take many hours to accomplish. In many cities, especially St. Catharines, and Waterloo, in Ontario, the media coordinator (sometimes called Public Information Officer), is to assist the Chief Administrative Officer in: preparing press releases and public education notices; making media kits, public service announcements and flyers; holding public meetings, issuing identification, preparing city officials for media briefings, conducting media tours, monitoring the media, and issuing accreditation badges to media. I've done many of these jobs for government and corporations and in the office of the world's longest-serving big city mayor. I've also tested the abilities of large corporations to do these jobs in elaborate simulations mobilizing hundreds of responders and costing hundreds of thousands of dollars. This work cannot be done well within a day by half a dozen people. Moreover, I called the city of Waterloo to ask who could issue me a media badge. No one had heard of this process, and no one has called me back.

Many plans list threats and risks. Baltimore has a section on public health. This section lists 35,000 cases of sexually transmitted diseases and 10,000 animal bites. All other categories are 1,000 or fewer. There's no mention of prevention. These 45,000 cases can be addressed and many prevented. That's what a good emergency manager does – not just wait for the ill effects before responding.

Most plans still have accessibility challenges. There is little point in looking at maps with no street names, small fonts, text which prints off the page, pop ups and drop downs which obscure text, or reading references to annexes that don't exist. Web-based communication is different than making a brochure or writing a letter.

Cleveland, Ohio, boasts that its plan is color coded for "convenience" and yet, on a black and white printer, this only creates oddly-shaded text.

Many plans take a stab at quantitative risk assessment (QRA). In Nashville's plan, it's noted that "the probability of dam failure is low and not predictable." But there have been 55 past failures and 21 partial failures. This tells me it's high and predictable. Like jargon, QRA techniques are mainly lost on the general public. Most are lost on me and I've trained in the area. Nashville notes "The terms '10-year,' '50-year,' '100-year,' and '500-year' floods are used to describe the estimated probability of a flood event happening in any given year. A 10-year flood has a 10 percent probability of occurring in any given year, a 50-year event a 2 percent probability, a 100- year event a 1 percent probability, and a 500-year event a 0.2 percent probability. While unlikely, it is possible to have two 100-or even 500-year floods within years or months of each other." At the end of these definitions, the main point to be taken might be to raise the hot water heater and appliances in your basement. That should be the first priority.

Also in Nashville, they define risk as equalling impact plus vulnerability times likelihood. For me, this means that risk may equal 2 dead (impact), plus high winds (to which we are vulnerable), times every 3 years (when winds are high). How does the average citizen calculate 2 + windy x 3?

Long Beach, California uses FEMA's Calculated Priority Risk Index (CPRI). This uses four categories for hazards and a weighting scheme. Here's the formula for an earthquake in Long Beach:

$$CPRI= [(3 \times 0.45) + (3 \times 0.30) + (4 \times 0.15) + (1 \times 0.10)] = 2.95.$$

Other hazards, such as Tsunami (2.55), windstorms (2.90), flooding (2.45) have what appear to be similar ratings, even if they've never occurred. What action should a reader take after this calculation? Or is the calculation, rather than mitigation, the desired result?

By the way, there's a serious justification for my criticism. Some British studies, examining 60 years of QRA results, note that events don't often happen the way quantitative analysis predicted. Take one current example to see why – the World Health Organization's prediction on the hundreds of millions who may die in a future influenza pandemic. It's hard to imagine the quantitative decision tree the WHO used, considering that the flu virus wasn't isolated in a lab until 15 years after the first pandemic which killed between 50 and 100 million people during and just after World War I. Some physicians and scientists thought the flu was spread by musty books. Since then we've had massive changes in public health, smoking cessation, air quality, building codes mandating sinks in bathrooms for hand washing, and many other changes. A current guess on this changing history is just a guess, not QRA.

On evacuation, we're still in a dangerous state. Charlotte, North Carolina, has a very useful academic article. It's not a plan and the city is not off the hook from doing the tough planning that will allow for a safe evacuation, but this information is a good start. The data on how difficult it is to get people to comply with evacuation orders, and the fact that a public preparedness program may not help is sobering. So is the notion of "shadow evacuation" – people near an evacuation zone who also leave, and spontaneous evacuations. Human behaviour is difficult to predict.

## More Bad News: No Standards or Clear Language

Despite a Presidential order in the US, and obvious need, there are few approaches or formats that we find are standard in emergency plans. Guelph, Ontario, acknowledges this, indicating, "...there has been a variance of approaches within Ontario, a lack of standardized tools to manage incidents, and hence no single province-wide system to ensure effective coordination." This is true in every jurisdiction. In Detroit, citizens are advised in the city's written plan to leave porch lights on if the home has been evacuated. This is a useless direction in a power outage, and will probably not be known by most citizens. If responders think this direction is in effect, they will miss people who need help, and waste time at the doors of empty homes. No wonder this is the only plan I've seen with this policy.

There is more jargon and more acronyms than we originally found. Several cities, including Baltimore, have a "turn around, don't drown" campaign, which could mean turn your back to surging water, which might cause death. I think they mean turn your car around and don't drive down a flooded street. This should be made clear. Oddly, in that city, SPW means Shelter in Place, EVE means Evacuation and TOE means there's a 911 outage. One can imagine the effects of police telling citizens there's a TOE, so don't bother calling for help.

Kansas City uses ARFF (Aircraft Rescue Firefighting) and has a TEW (Terrorism Early Warning Group). It's easy to imagine the confusion if a police officer warns citizens that the TEW has called out the ARFF for fear the fires were set by terrorists. Often, when I ask for the meaning of an acronyms that have been used for years, many people have long forgotten.

Buffalo, New York, features an observation about the management of an emergency. That city plan states: "A central focal point of analytical and coordinative planning skills which could obtain the necessary political leadership and backing when needed, is required to coordinate the programs and agencies necessary to bring about a high quality of recovery and community redevelopment." While reading this unfocussed ramble, people could be dying and response may have stopped.

While not jargon, unnecessary definitions slow down response. Philadelphia defines the term "notification" as "to make known or inform..." and the term "notify" as "to inform about a condition, event or situation." Kitchener, Ontario defines "Police Chief." It's hard to imagine competing definitions.

Unexplored solutions still leap off the pages of these plans. Several cities use computer modeling to estimate the hundreds of thousands of tons of debris that will be left by a storm or flood, and the thousands of truck loads required to clear the streets. Most of this debris will be from trees, so the obvious solution is to prune the trees. This is good for the trees, can help prevent limbs from falling on power lines and helps in many other ways. In at least one city, the direction is to estimate the number of chords of wood that are blocking streets. This is an almost impossible task, even for someone who has chopped and piled lots of cordwood, as I have. Worse, it's a waste of time when what's needed is clear roads. Kansas City uses common sense by stating its "70-Hour-Push" is designed to clear roadways "as soon as practical and will not be delayed to develop debris estimates or conduct other assessment activities."

Few cities have dealt with the communications component of emergency planning as well as Long Beach, California. The advice for spokespeople is prudent (don't speculate, everything is on the record, etc.) and the tips on making messages (using the 5Ws) is simple and effective. Houston wisely points out the mutual interests of both reporters and emergency responders.

Most plans rightly try to rank emergencies by severity. This gives responders and the public a good idea of how bad things are. In most cities, emergencies are ranked Level I, Level II and Level III with the third level being the worst. But in London, Ontario, it's the exact opposite, with Level III being the lowest and Level I being the highest or worst, which may actually make more sense. Buffalo, New York, has two levels. Pittsburgh has four, and four is the worst. Louisville also has four levels with one being the worst. Louisville also uses the three level coast guard MARSEC rating and the three level hazardous material rating. Edmonton has four levels with four being the worst. Austin has seven levels with one being catastrophic, but the numerals 7 and 1 look alike. Tuscon's threat level is colour coded. Houston has both color coding, numbers and a combination of both. Indianapolis doesn't seem to have levels but their plan has four parts. Columbus has a medallion or seal with the heading "Ready in 3." I can't find the 3 things. I fear a conversation among emergency responders who are all talking past each other on how bad their emergency is because they have different terminology. However, perhaps my fear is moot because, with limited interoperability, it's unlikely that responders from different jurisdictions trying to trigger a mutual aid agreement could actually communicate with each other on emergency frequencies.

I now understand a little better why plans are so vague and feature jargon, acronyms and lists of contributors. Most jurisdictions have portions of their plans which are secret. This makes sense. We don't need to know where the police keep their secret stashes of weapons, or if there are underground storage tanks of fuel or water hidden somewhere. But, most jurisdictions have a law requiring cities to have written plans, update them annually and make the results known to the public. One result of this double life that emergency plans have is public confusion. I'm sometimes not sure if I'm looking at the city's plan, a summary of it or an old plan. Some appendices and schedules are confidential but referenced regularly in the public portion of the plan.

In Mississauga, legal jargon adds to the confusion. The plan I found "...forms Schedule "A" to the current City of Mississauga Emergency Management By-law (see appendix S)..." So, the plan is a schedule (attachment) to a By-law. I don't think we can see the By-laws because "The Plan's appendices are confidential and are not to be made public..." Are the plan's appendices the same as the By-law's appendices, and if so, is the whole plan secret, contrary to provincial statute?

## What's Needed

I am struck by the simple things we'll need in an emergency. Chain saws, shovels, pick up trucks, snow ploughs, buses, regular cars, crowbars, snowmobiles, and regular people to operate all this stuff will save lives and money. I've been waiting to read a plan that has an inventory of such things and people, including retired workers, bus drivers, and heavy equipment operators. As I read my 50th plan my eyes lit up. In Barrie, Ontario's plan, page 45, item 6.11, there is a big heading--HUMAN RESOURCES DEVELOPMENT CANADA (HRDC). Under the heading there are six bullet points listing the assistance that the local office of the federal ministry can provide during an emergency. This help includes "paid workers and volunteers...the capability of employers in the affected area to resume operation, re-deployment of former workers" and other matters.

My first thought was that this is new and not in any other emergency plan I've read. My second thought was that this is very valuable. My third thought was that this is not true. I tried to call the Barrie office of HRDC and spent about two hours on the phone over two days with government officials in Ottawa and Toronto who told me how HRDC had changed to ESDC and that Service Canada was the operating arm of ESDC. All this is irrelevant, of course. If you're in a SNAFU, you need help PDQ and ASAP, not acronyms. Not only did I waste two hours, but I was not provided a phone number and was told that the federal government would refer such a request back to the city which has the appropriate workers. I told the patient civil servant that if I were still working for a mayor and called the federal government for assistance and 2 hours later they called me and told me to provide that assistance to myself, there might be dead people, and certainly hell to pay. This reference in Barrie's plan was wishful thinking, a misunderstanding, or made up, but never tested or updated since 2008.

# Some Wonderful Examples

In some cities, common sense has prevailed. Houston has estimates of how many portable toilets and hand washing stations may be needed. Kansas City acknowledges that "mutual aid resources will be minimal..." I'm a big fan of mutual aid (as in California), sharing recourses, lists of suppliers and memoranda of understanding. But the reality is that your emergency may affect those people you're hoping will help. But some in Kansas City know the need to plan for these let downs. There's a "Plan Bulldozer" set up by the private sector construction industry. "Its purpose is to meet the need for equipment and expertise from the area's construction companies to alleviate human suffering and loss of property caused by natural and man-made disasters." This is brilliant and will save lives. The wild goose chase in Barrie won't help.

Speaking of Kansas City's plan, they get off on the right foot. Many plans have positive civic messages more suited to a Kiwanis luncheon speech than a crisis plan. Kansas City engages in what the military would call an "appreciation" and others might call threat or risk analysis, or a situation analysis. Kansas City has two major rivers, levees and barge lines. There are 600 daily freight arrivals and departures, and the city is first in America in tonnage and second in number of rail cars passing through (much like Sudbury in Canada). The Federal government is the largest employer with the Federal Reserve Bank, IRS, and other offices. Fort Leavenworth and several military facilities are nearby, including the country's only B-2 stealth bomber base. That's all you need to know to take a good guess at the risks facing the city.

Kansas City then starts where I started – with New Orleans. The Kansas City plan states that New Orleans "failed to provide adequate transportation for citizens without their own vehicular transportation," and traffic overwhelmed evacuation routes. The plan notes that there is almost no advice from the federal or state governments on evacuation, and the best is in a 1984 FEMA document. This is not, as the expression goes, close enough for government work.

The plan in Kansas City is strong on data to help plan an evacuation. It lists numbers of buses and numbers of drivers (as does Sacramento's evacuation plan). Buses outnumber drivers, and will thus sit idle. It lists the number of people downtown at night and during the day, along with estimated numbers of tourists. All a planner has to do is a little math to see how smoothly an evacuation would go at a particular time of day. The plan has a realistic prediction that it might take four hours to evacuate.

If people are in danger, for whatever reason, emergency responders should make plans to keep them safer.

A big risk, which is ignored, is pets. People will put themselves in danger for their pets. They will return to evacuated neighborhoods for pets. They will have a hard time getting pets into shelters, hotels or motels. Most people don't have an emergency plan for their pets. "One-third of dog owners feel closer to their dogs than to any human family member," according to Kansas City's plan.

But Kansas City rises to these challenges. Their plan has an inventory of pet cats and dogs as well as stray animals. It lists locations and facilities that can take in pets. It lists hotels and motels that will accept pets, and has a plan for pet owners to tend to their animals in pet shelters. There are pre-written announcements with advice for caring for pets. There are also lists of methods of disposing of dead pets – an important public health issue.

This plan tells me that the swash-buckling crisis manager who swoops in after the damage is done is too highly prized. The risk manger who prevents an emergency is unsung. City emergency plans focus too much on response, obtaining grants, or aspirational goals, and not enough on prevention. We can strengthen our buildings against earthquakes and high winds, plant trees to reduce flooding, replace hard surfaces with vegetation for the same effect, reduce the ill effects of heat with light coloured roofs, and take other preventive measures. These measures are not discussed much in emergency plans.

# I'M MAD (angry)

And where does this epilogue and book end? In many ways it doesn't and can't. It can't end because there's too much work left to do. This is a bigger project than I thought. I began on my own more than ten years ago. Then I enlisted the help of a small group of bright students, beginning two years ago. In two rounds of printing and reading, I've studied about 8,000 pages of emergency plans and a few hundred academic studies on the topic.

And why all this work? I think of a quote variously attributed to George Bernard Shaw and Robert F. Kennedy – some people "see things as they are and say why? I dream things that never were and say why not?" I suppose I'm asking both of these questions, and perhaps aggrandizing my project. When many people ask why or why not, they take some action. They join a non-governmental organization like the one I met with in New York, and they try to help. Others rise to the top of the corporate world like the man who advocates using social media to tell people there's no power. Others join a charity, become a civic official or a Scout troop leader. What I do is

get mad. I get mad at the jargon, the old plans, the pages of definition, the pages left intentionally blank, the secret appendices, and all the other matters raised in this book.

I've been critical in this book. I've used humour and even mockery in my syndicated columns to draw attention to the failings of our emergency plans. My view is that I need to use whatever techniques are available to get the attention and action of politicians, emergency planners, the police, firefighters, academics and all those with a portion of responsibility for the state of these plans. This matter is in their hands now, and I'll do all I can in print, social, and electronic media to cause them to take action.

When I was a young teenager, like many my age, I read J.D. Salinger's book, The Catcher in the Rye. That was a long time ago, but Mr. Antolini's advice to Holden Caulfield stuck with me. The influential teacher, with a mixed reputation, told Holden that he needed to decide if he was going to get enough education to see a sign in a fruit store reading "Apple's" and get mad at the incorrect use of the possessive case, or get mad enough to do something about it. I've admitted to being mad. Let's see if I've done something about what makes me mad.

# About the Author

Allan Bonner has spent his life studying cities. This research began as a boy, listening to his father, Harold Bonner, discuss pioneering the apartment–hotel concept for Montreal's Expo '67, Vancouver's early attempt at waterfront redevelopment – "Project 200," and then Harold's dramatic transformation of the Halifax–Dartmouth waterfront as head of the Halifax Waterfront Development Corporation. He saw Toronto's bank tower boom and then the condo boom decades later, and continued to hear wonderful private tutorials from his father who was involved in both.

After graduate school, Allan worked for the world's longest–serving big–city mayor – the charismatic and extremely popular Mel Lastman of North York. Then, as a consultant, Allan travelled up to 150 days per year on five continents for 30 years – always keeping an eye on urban issues.

While conducting research for this book, Allan lived for brief times in a privatised counsel flat in London, a sixth floor walk up in le Marais in Paris, and in Geneva. He has also travelled to cities on five continents to ride the monorail in Sydney, Vancouver's Skytrain, Chicago's people mover, the Chunnel to Brussels and Paris, the Star Ferry in Hong Kong, the Roosevelt Island tram in New York, the San Francisco cable car, the antique streetcars in Memphis, passenger trains across most of North America, high–speed rail in Europe and the bullet trains in Japan, trains in Eastern Europe, Australia and China, and a little that's left of the Orient Express. He also drove the Confederation Bridge, the highways of Europe and Robert Moses' parkways.

Allan has consulted on some of the major issues of our time – urban amalgamation, major sports stadiums, downtown revitalisation, waste management, and co–location of civic amenities. He has worked with military planners during and after the Cold War and 9/11, crisis planners before and after the Exxon Valdez oil spill, economic planners on OECD and G20 initiatives, and nuclear planners who use a 10 year time–line and 100,000 drawings to achieve their ends.

# Endnotes

1. The author is indebted to Senator Eggleton for the idea of electric cars feeding power back into the grid.

2 Hopkins, p. 12. On the environmental benefits of HSR, see J. Campos, & G. de Rus, "Some stylized facts about high–speed rail: A review of HSR experiences around the world." (Transport Policy), 2009, p. 25 See Moshe Givoni & David Bannister, "Role of the Railways in the Future of Air Transport", (Transportation Planning and Technology, February 2007, Vol. 30, No 1) on rail replacing one leg of what was once a two–flight journey, p. 97 and reducing the need for parking, p. 99, and "hands free" luggage transfer between modes, p. 101.

3 Note that Hopkins, p. 3, points out that the length of many airplane trips actually increased in the last 40 years of the 20th century, with most of the time being spent on the ground. See also A. Pita, P.F. Lopez, A. Teixiera, Bachiller, C. Casas–Esplugas and R. Sina, "Iberian rail: adding a new dimension to international travel, proceedings of the Institution of Civil Engineers", (Transport 161, Issue TR 2, paper 700039), p. 79 on TGV replacing airline routes.

4 Campos & de Rus, p. 26.

5 Mark Osbaldeston, *Unbuilt Toronto: A History of the City That Might Have Been*, (Toronto, ON: Dundurn Press), 2008, p. 127. Robert Millward cited the longer ferry, essentially a floating bridge coming into use, and is a supporter of the island airport. He also notes there is a generation of quieter and more fuel efficient jets. Chris Hume notes that it is a contentious issue, but that the Toronto Star editorially supports the facility.

6 The author toured this facility and is recounting these facts from memory.

7 Report on Energy Supply and Demand in Canada published by Statistics Canada. <http://www.statcan.gc.ca/pub/57-003-x/2007000/part-partie1-eng.htm>. The author was originally hoping for a decrease in nuclear, but Senator Eggleton indicated this as unrealistic.

8 On the energy savings possible from the monorail, see Hopkins, p. 8. An undeveloped theme is the connection between symbol, such as the monorail, and progress, in high technology. One wonders about the connections between Boeing in Seattle, the 1962 World's Fair, Microsoft and such.

9 See Kunstler, p. 117, on the value of garage apartments and apartments over stores. Katrina cottages are available at Lowe's. Granny flats are sometimes called garden apartments. The author played a role in promoting the award winning codicil home for CMHC. The latter had limited connections to city services and a vegetable garden. See also P. Bedford, *Steering the Good Ship Intensification*, (The Ontario Planning Journal, 20(4): 17-18), 2005, p. 1.

10 The author personally timed stair walking in the 13 story District Lofts building at Richmond & Spadina when he lived there.

11 See Kunstler on the "one–sided street," p. 184.

12 The author was peripherally involved in the site selection of the Domed Stadium and notes that the site was criticized for a lack of parking and egress.

13 Jacobs might add bike washing, pig roasts and "Italian street festivals", p. 110.

14 Reported on the Science Daily website on October 1 2009 "Horticultural Scientists Develop Slow–growing Grass" http://www.sciencedaily.com/videos/2008/1009–slower_growing_grass.htm.

15 See Osbaldeston, p. 43, on Fuller's "Pro–To Cities."

16 See Osbaldeston, p. 53, on Harbour City.

17 Senator Eggleton points out that the Don would need to be cleaned up considerably before house boat use would be palatable. This echoes Dr. Woznow's input.

18 Osbaldeston, p. 107.

19 This idea arose out of the state run collective vacation spots used in East Germany. The author visited displays on this topic in the GDR museum in Berlin.

20 See Jacobs for the use of the terms border, p. 257, barrier, p. 259, how they divide cities, p. 264, and their morphing into "a seam rather than a barrier," p. 267–8.

21 Jacobs, p. 383, quoting Lynch. See also the role of landmarks, p. 384.

22 See Bedford, *All about Mixed Use*, (The Ontario Planning Journal, (24)4: 20–22), 2009, p. 1. The author has used and viewed these facilities.

23 See L. Rochon CitySpace column, The Globe and Mail, July 8, 2009. p. R2 for Les Klein's alternatative view of parkland on the Gardiner.

24 See P. Bedford, *Go Bold or Go Home* (The Ontario Planning Journal, (23)3: 28–29), 2008. p. 2 on modeling with the assumption of "no new road construction."

25 The author has discussed the issue of public washrooms with Robert Millward apart from the formal interview for this project. He identified heating as one of the major obstacles to providing public washrooms.

26 Informal conversation with Terry White, Ministry of Education on this initiative in Saskatchewan.

27 The author has ridden and viewed the vintage street cars in Memphis.

28 Marincioni, Fausto & Federica Appiotti, The Lyon–Turin High Speed Rail: The Public Debate and Perception of Environmental Risk in Susa Valley, Italy, *Environmental Management (2009)* 43:871 on the use of right–of–ways. Even those interviewed for this paper who express concerns about monorails in neighbourhoods (Messers Hume and Eggleton especially) indicate that using railway and road rights of way is attractive.

29 See Hopkins, p. 4, on the detriment of steel wheels, and p. 5 on the linear induction motor.

30 A. Hedelin, O. Bunketorp and U. Björnstig, "Public transport in metropolitan areas – a danger for unprotected road users." (Safety Science, Volume 40, Issue 5, July) 2002. Millward seems to agree.

31 The fundraising aspect is Dr. Woznow's idea.

32 McQuaid, p. 194–197.

33 Hopkins, p. 7.

34 The author has worked both on staff and as a consultant for TVO, and consulted to several relevant ministries, and the ROM and has reason to believe that such interagency cooperation would be supported and possible.

35 Chris Hume favours infrastructure that serves two purposes. He notes that a street is both a destination and a transport system.

36 See Bedford, *Go Bold or Go Home*, p. 2 on the need for "new revenue menus from both the public and private sector" and modeling for the "true cost of transportation choices" and *Steering the Good Ship Intensification*, p. 2 on all levels of government needing to "develop a full A to Z list of carrots and sticks" to achieve intensification.

37 The first of which was the gas tax, as implemented in Vancouver. See Harcourt, p. 161.

38 For a captivating recounting of the former see Caro, p. 525–566. For HSR's sources of funding see California High Speed Rail Authority, *California High–Speed Train Business Plan*, (Sacramento, CA), 2008, p. 4.

39 On the need for support from all levels of government, see Bonner, Harcourt, p. 9, 23, 50, 103.

40 Informal discussion with Robert Millward.

41 See J.P. Arduin, *Development and Economic Evaluation of High Speed in France*, (Japan Railway & Transport Review, 26–31), 1994, p. 30 on ridership rises in general, p. 31 on the reduction of airplane and road use. See also P. Coto–Millan, V. Inglada, and B. Rey, *Effects of network economies in high–speed rail: the Spanish case*, (Annals of Regional Science, 911–925), 2007, p. 918 on HSR increasing both frequency and overall ridership.

42 Arduin, p. 26.

43 The author has worked with at least one pharmaceutical company which is trying to obtain drug funding from both labour and revenue ministries because of the benefit to the general treasury of getting workers back to work through drug therapy. See also Arduin, p. 29, on the value of the individual's time as a cost. See Coto–Millan et. al., p. 912, on reduced travel time being a social benefit and externalities including "pollution, noise, accidents and congestion" on p. 913.

44 Robert Millward indicates this may be a key to success.

45 Hopkins, p. 2 and on the safety of the monorail, p. 5, on container freight as revenue source, p. 12. Note that Campos & de Rus cite the case of freight services using "the spare capacity of high–speed lines during the night." See also Campos & de Rus on the economic viability of HSR. Senator Eggleton has pointed out that Go Transit shares a line with freight, but also indicates on high–speed, long distance lines, there should be separation.

46 California High Speed Raul Authority, p. 9. See also Campos & de Rus on "sunk costs" which some might term path dependency.

47 Mike Woods, Saskatchewan's Crown Investments Corporation, informal discussion.

48 Ronald Hirshhorn, *Transport Canada, The Estimation of Road Wear and Capital Costs*, 6/1/2009. p. 2, 9, 36, 42 and Kunstler, p. 90–91. See also Jane Jacobs on separating types of traffic in both time and space, p. 346. On her version of using the monorail for freight, see "post–officing" on the same page. On the "[E]rosion of cities by automobiles", p. 349, and 352 for the struggle between access by cars and public transport service. On "attrition" of automobiles, see p. 363. Jacobs and this paper agree that if driving is less convenient, less driving will occur, p. 366.

49 Hirshhorn, p. 14.

50 Hirshhorn, p. 14.

51 On the connection between scale and speed, see Kuntsler, p. 116.

52 Note the model for the monorail in Hopkins, p. 8.

53 Both Rollo Myers and Senator Eggleton have pointed out that density transfers over long distances can be controversial and create too much density on one area, Senator Eggleton holds out the possibility that collaboration among cultural agencies and educational institutions on this issue might be workable.

54 See Jacobs on vendors, p. 396.

55 Co–location of multiple services is being investigated in Regina by Terry White of the Ministry of Education and the author has had private conversations on this topic with Mr. White. The notion has been supported for about one hundred years by practitioners from Mary Parker Follett to Dr. Bette Stephenson, when the latter was in the Ontario cabinet.

56 Robert Millward who has worked with those responsible.

57 Bedford, *All about Mixed Use*, p. 1.

58 See Marincioni & Appiotti, p. 865, on "transparency…among the project's various stakeholders" and p. 874, on risk perception and communication as a catalyst for consensus on building large infrastructure. Senator Eggleton has pointed out the difficulty of increasing density on Danforth Avenue and indicates incentives need to be explored to motivate multiple land–owners. This paper does not assert that the incentives discussed are exhaustive or are the ones that will work. They are just an exploration of ways and means.

59 Rollo Myers pointed out that the police wanted a much larger site elsewhere and lobbied against using repurposed historic building.

60 On the need for private sector operation of transit, see Hopkins, p. 8 and p. 11 for public support. On the limits of seeking public support, see C. Lindblom, "The Science of 'Muddling Through'", (Public Administration Review 19: 79–88 [Campbell and Fainstein, 288–304]), 1959, p. 80. See Pita, et. al. on the role of the private sector.

61 A. Loeb, *The Condominium Act: A User's Manual (2nd Edition)*, (Toronto, ON: Thomson Canada Ltd.), 2005, p. 58–62.

62 Appreciation of citizens' land and buildings might be a start. See Bedford, *All about Mixed Use*, p. 2.

# Appendices

## MOST ADEQUATE PLANS

These plans were written clearly, with little to no jargon/abstract language, are relevant to regular citizens, and/or are accessible in different languages/font–sizes (alphabetical order).

- Burlington/Oakville/Milton (shared), ON
- Calgary, AB
- Las Vegas (Las Vegas County plan), NV
- Los Angeles (Los Angeles county), CA
- Manchester, UK
- Mississauga, ON
- Portland, OR
- Richmond, BC
- Saskatoon, SK
- St. Catharines, ON

## BEST WEBSITE RESOURCES

These websites promote downloadable content, are printer friendly, offer links to contact city officials, methods to get involved, are well organized, have large fonts, language options have real–time emergency feeds, and/or links to social media (alphabetical order).

- Austin, TX
- Boston, MA
- Kansas City, MS
- Los Angeles City, CA
- Mississauga, ON
- New York, NY
- Portland, OR
- Regina, SK
- Windsor, ON
- Winnipeg, MA

## USE OF COMMUNICATION TOOLS

These cities promote means other than conventional email/radio/telephone to notify the public of an emergency.

- Leeds, UK – Leeds has a police helicopter that assists in evacuations and communicating with the public during an emergency; the program is called "sky shout."

- Louisville, KN – Outdoor warning sirens and loudspeakers allow emergency vehicles to communicate necessary information to the public during an emergency.

- Fort Worth and Dallas, TX – Outdoor warning sirens that notify the public are tested weekly, 149 sirens for Fort Worth, and 94 for Dallas, are strategically located across the city.

- Detroit, MI – Door-to-door patrol is used when necessary, in addition to outdoor warning sirens.

# COMMUNITY ENGAGEMENT

These cities have citizens involved beyond traditional volunteering.

- Memphis, TN – Memphis offers a two–day comprehensive course that is free, covers disaster preparedness, which includes fire suppression, light search and rescue, and terrorism.

- Seattle, WA – Seattle has a partnership with Target 2–hour emergency preparedness workshop that includes emergency preparedness kit and a starter kit; participants receive a $50.00 gift card for families that attend.

- Portland, OR – Portland offers a great volunteer program that falls under the CERT (Community Emergency Response Team) designation by FEMA (Federal Emergency Management Agency). Unlike many volunteer programs however, Portland requires police background checks for all their volunteers.

- Surrey, BC –Surrey holds the "Shakeout" program, which is Canada's largest earthquake simulation. Surrey also holds monthly neighbourhood emergency preparation meetings.

- Vancouver, BC – Vancouver offers free emergency workshops for families, businesses, and communities. The city also participates in the "Shakeout" program referenced above under Surrey, BC.

- Mississauga, ON – Mississauga holds a 5–day summer camp for 14–17 year olds. This city also has an interactive game for children on their website that teaches them about emergency preparedness.

# LONGEST PLANS

- Fort Worth, TX (680+)
- Pittsburgh, PN (550+)
- San Diego County, CA (450+)
- Oklahoma City, OK (350+)
- Philadelphia, PN (350+)
- Sacramento, CA (250+)
- Fresno, CA (230+)
- Richmond, BC (210+)
- Brisbane, AU (200+)
- Kansas City, KN (161+)

## MOST RECENT

Plans ordered from most recent onwards.

- Portland, OR, last updated 2014
- Ottawa, ON, updates regularly, last update 2013
- Brisbane, AU, updated 2013
- Vancouver, BC, last updated October 2013
- New York City, NY, last updated 2013
- Toronto, ON, last updated 2013
- Sudbury, ON, last updated February 2013
- Hamilton, ON, last updated February 2013
- Birmingham, UK, last updated 2013
- New Orleans, LO, last updated October 2013, but not open to the public to view

## MOST DATED

Plans ranked from from 2008 or older fell in this category. Organized oldest to least–old (as of September 2013 when this project started).

- Halifax, NS, last updated 1996
- Cape Breton, NS, last updated 2001
- Washington, DC, last updated 2002
- Oklahoma, OK, last updated 2006
- Pittsburgh, PN, last updated 2006
- Oshawa, ON, last updated 2006
- San Antonio, TX, last updated 2006
- Tampa, FL, last updated 2007
- Fresno, CA, last updated 2008
- Sacramento, CA, last updated 2008
- Barrie, ON, last updated 2008
- San Francisco, CA, last updated 2008
- Forth Worth, TX, last updated 2008
- Columbus, OH, last updated 2008

## CITIES LACKING DOWNLOADABLE EMERGENCY PREPAREDNESS CONTENT (as of June 2014)

- Syracuse, NY
- Rochester, NY
- Fredericton, NB
- Red Deer, AB
- Liverpool, UK

## ACTIVE SOCIAL MEDIA PRESENCE

These cities have more than a general city social network page; they have a dedicated emergency preparedness page and they have at least bi–weekly emergency preparedness related updates (as of June 2014).

- Pittsburg, PN
- Austin, TX
- Tucson, AZ
- Toronto, ON
- Atlanta, GA
- Onondaga County (Syracuse), NY
- New Orleans, LA
- New York, NY
- Washington, DC
- Halifax, NS
- Guelph, ON
- San Antonio, TX
- Portland, OR
- Jacksonville, FL
- Nashville, TN
- Louisville, KN
- Sacramento, CA
- San Diego, CA
- Oklahoma City, OK
- Los Angeles, CA
- Long Beach, CA
- Memphis, TN
- Orlando, FL
- San Francisco, CA
- Houston, TX
- Indianapolis, IL
- Baltimore, MA
- Las Vegas, NV
- Miami, FL
- El Paso, TX
- Boston, MA
- Chicago, IL
- Charlotte, NC
- Columbus, OH
- Kansas City, KS

## OTHER CITIES THAT DO NOT HAVE ACCEPTABLE VOLUNTEER PROGRAMS TO ENGAGE THE PUBLIC (as of June 2014)

- Quebec City, QC
- Charlotte, NC
- Buffalo, NY
- Melbourne, AU
- Louisville, KN
- Fredericton, NB
- Liverpool, UK
- Edmonton, AB
- North Vancouver, BC
- Calgary, AB
- St. Catharines, ON
- Windsor, ON
- Leeds, UK
- London, UK
- Bradford, UK
- Glasgow, UK
- Cape Breton, NS
- Birmingham, UK
- Red Deer, AB
- Moncton, BC,
- Halifax, NS
- Montreal, QC
- Regina, SK

## CERT PROGRAM:

The Community Emergency Response Team (CERT) is a volunteer program led by FEMA. This program educates the public about disaster preparedness for hazards they may face in case of emergency. This program includes basic disaster response skills training in fire safety, search and rescue, team organization and disaster medical response.

- Memphis, TN
- Dallas, TX
- Fort Worth, TX
- Austin, TX
- Houston, TX
- Indianapolis, IL
- Detroit, MI
- Denver, CO
- Boston, MA
- Kansas city, MS
- Pittsburgh, PN
- Albuquerque, NM
- Phoenix, AZ
- Tucson, AZ
- Tampa, FL
- Rochester, NY
- San Diego, CA
- Fresno, CA

## PLANS WITH 10–POINT FONT OR SMALLER

"Printed Website" refers webpages that are printed directly off the website (e.g. a website homepage that provides an introduction to the city's emergency management). Unless stated otherwise, the remainder of the cities had 10–point font or less in their downloaded and printed plans (as of June 2014).

- San Diego, CA
- Louisville, KN
- Phoenix, AZ
- Austin, TX
- Atlanta, GA
- Manchester, UK
- North Vancouver, BC (Printed Website)
- Liverpool, UK (Printed Website)
- Dallas, TX
- Detroit, MI
- Quebec City, QC
- Boston, MA (Small font was found at various times the "ready Boston" printed emergency guide)
- Columbus, OH (Printed Website)
- Chicago, IL (Small font was found in the "alert Chicago" emergency brochure)
- Barrie, ON
- Buffalo, NY

## CITIES WITH ADJUSTABLE FONT ON WEBSITE OR EMERGENCY PLAN (as of June 2014)

- San Diego, CA
- Sydney, AU
- Toronto, ON
- Birmingham, UK
- Oshawa, ON
- Moncton, NB
- St. John's, NL
- Greater Sudbury, ON
- Thunder Bay, ON
- Victoria, BC
- Burnaby, BC
- New York, NY
- Burlington, ON
- London, ON
- Portland, OR
- Richmond, BC
- Brisbane, AU
- Nashville, TN
- Louisville, KN
- Oklahoma, OK
- Boston, MA
- Melbourne, AU
- San Francisco, CA

# CITIES WITH NOTABLY USEFUL VIDEOS (as of June 2014)

Vancouver, BC – (Earthquakes) https://www.youtube.com/watch?v=Bq1VHnq0Yvk

New York, NY – (General Preparedness information for NYC) https://www.youtube.com/watch?v=bn-PiFzE5qXQ&feature=youtu.be

Mississauga, ON– ("buzz bytes" general emergency preparation series) https://www.youtube.com/watch?v=eN7uK9zbtJ8&feature=c4–overview&list=UUxpfoR5ujQ90fDTKRQj3TyQ

San Jose, CA – (disaster service workers) http://cchealth.org/emergencies/video–disaster.php

St. John NL; Burnaby BC; and Montreal QC Link to Canadian Gov. – (General Preparedness) http://www.getprepared.gc.ca/cnt/rsrcs/vds/mkng–pln–eng.aspx

San Antonio, TX – (General Preparedness) https://www.youtube.com/watch?v=DqfkQ6pwf84

Edmonton, AB – (Emergency Alert Series) https://www.youtube.com/watch?v=qc8PUy6kjv0

Fort Worth, TX – (Terrorism and shooting awareness) https://www.youtube.com/watch?v=5Vc-SwejU2D0&feature=youtu.be

Dallas, TX – (Terrorism and shooting awareness) https://www.youtube.com/watch?v=5Vc-SwejU2D0&feature=youtu.be

Detroit, MI – (General Preparedness) http://www.detroitmi.gov/DepartmentsandAgencies/HomelandSecurityEmergencyManagement/EmergencyPreparedness.aspx

Boston, MA – (General Preparedness) http://www.cityofboston.gov/cable/video_library.asp?ID=1374

Kansas City, MS – (CERT volunteer preparedness) http://www.preparemetrokc.org/Get_Involved/certrodeo.asp

# Bibliography

Amery, M. and J. Lord. (2006). MLA Review Committee on Secondary Suites: Final Report. Government of Alberta. Retrieved from http://www.municipalaffairs.alberta.ca/documents/ss/MLA_Final_Report_Secondary_Suites.pdf

Andrews, J. (March 2005). Not your Grandmother's Granny Flat. *Planning*, 71:3, 8–9.

Canada Mortgage and Housing Corporation. (n.d.). Secondary Suites. Retrieved from: http://www.cmhc–schl.gc.ca/en/co/renoho/refash/refash_040.cfm

City of Abbotsford. (n.d.) Secondary Suites: Frequently Asked Questions. Retrieved from http://www.abbotsford.ca/Assets/Abbotsford/Dev+Services+–+Planning+and+Environment/Development+Brochures/Secondary+Suites.pdf

City of Abbotsford. (April 2011). Secondary Suites: Technical Requirements for Construction of Accessory Secondary Suites in the City of Abbotsford. Retrieved from http://www.abbotsford.ca/Assets/Abbotsford/Dev+Services+–+Building+ Department/ Secondary+Suites/ Technical+Requirements+for+Secondary+Suites.pdf

City of Calgary. (November 2011). Secondary Suites: A Guide to Developing a Secondary Suite. Retrieved from http://www.calgary.ca/PDA/DBA/Documents/brochures/secondary_suites_brochure.pdf

City of Calgary. (November 2011). Secondary Suites: Alberta Building Code Requirements. Retrieved from http://www.calgary.ca/PDA/DBA/Documents/brochures/secondary_suites_abc_requirements.pdf

City of Calgary. (n.d). Secondary Suites 101 – Getting Started. Retrieved from http://www.calgary.ca/CS/OLSH/Documents/Affordable–housing/Enterprise–Housing–Program/Secondary–suites/Secondary%20Suites%20Grant%20Program%20Brochure.pdf

City of Coquitlam. (n.d.) Secondary Suites. Retrieved from http://www.coquitlam.ca/planning–and–development/resources/secondary–suites.aspx

City of Coquitlam. (2012). Zoning Bylaw. Retrieved from http://www.coquitlam.ca/city-hall/bylaws/frequently-requested/Zoning-Bylaw.aspx

City of Kelowna. (2010, May 12). Bulletin Number 10-01: Secondary Suite (Legalization or Decommission). Retrieved from http://www.kelowna.ca/CityPage/Docs/PDFs//Inspection%20Services/Bulletins/Secondary%20Suite%20%28Legalization%20or%20Decommission%29.pdf

City of Kelowna. (2010-2011). Consolidated Zoning Bylaw No. 8000: Section 12 – Rural Residential Zones. Retrieved from http://www.kelowna.ca/CityPage/Docs/PDFs//Bylaws/Zoning%20Bylaw%20No.%208000/Section%2012%20-%20Rural%20Residential%20Zones.pdf

City of Kelowna. (2011, December 19). Draft Resolution re: Secondary Suites. Retrieved from http://www.kelowna.ca/CityPage/Docs/PDFs%5C%5CCouncil%5CMeetings%5CCouncil%20Meetings%202012%5C2012-01-09%5CItem%207.1%20-%20Draft%20Resolution,%20Secondary%20Suites.pdf

City of Kelowna. (2004, August 5). Memorandum: Proposed Bylaw Amendments for Secondary Suites in Accessory Buildings. Retrieved from http://www.kelowna.ca/CityPage/Docs/PDFs%5C%5CCouncil%5CMeetings%5CCouncil%20Meetings%202003%5C2003-12-16%5CPublic%20Hearing%5CItem%203.4%20-%20BL%209119%20-%20TA03-0010%20-%20Zoning%20Bylaw%20Amendments%20re%20Secondary%20Suites%20in%20Accessory%20Buildings.pdf

City of Kelowna. (2003, December 11). Text Amendment No. TA03-0010 – A Bylaw to Amend the Regulations for Secondary Suites in Accessory Buildings. Retrieved from http://www.kelowna.ca/CityPage/Docs/PDFs%5C%5CCouncil%5CMeetings%5CCouncil%20Meetings%202003%5C2003-12-16%5CRegular%20Meeting%5CItem%205.3%20-%20BL9119%20-%20TA03-0010%20-%20Zoning%20Bylaw%20Amendments%20-%20Secondary%20Suites%20in%20Accessory%20Buildings.pdf

City of Langley. (n.d.). Secondary Suites Program: Information Brochure. Retrieved from: http://www.city.langley.bc.ca/images/Brochures/secondary_suites_brochure.pdf

City of Langley. (2006, October 16). Secondary Suites Study: Final Report. Retrieved from: http://www.city.langley.bc.ca/images/Reports/secondary_suites_report.pdf

City of Vancouver. (2004, January 13). Policy Report: Development and Building, Subject: Secondary Suites. Retrieved from http://vancouver.ca/ctyclerk/cclerk/20040301/p2.pdf

City of Vancouver. (2012). Secondary Suite Program. Retrieved from http://vancouver.ca/commsvcs/licandinsp/compliance/bylawadmin/pdf/sspguide.pdf

Copeletti, J. Phone Interview. Sales Manager at Titan Mobile Homes (a division of Champion Homes). 10 May 2010, 4:00 PM.

Koebel, C.T. et al. (October 2003*). Evaluation of the HUD Elder Cottage Housing Opportunity (ECHO)Program.* Blacksburg, Virginia: Virginia Polytechnic Institute and State University. Prepared for US Department of Housing and Urban Development, Office of Policy Development and Research.

Earhart, C.C. (1999). Attitudes of Housing Professionals toward Residential Options for the Elderly. *Journal of Housing for the Elderly,* 13:1-2, 65-78.

Goodman, J. (2003, August 4). Florida's Granny-flat flop. *Governing Magazine,* 44.

Government of New South Wales. (n.d.) Supporting Affordable Rental Housing – Granny Flats (Secondary Dwellings). Retrieved from http://www.planning.nsw.gov.au/LinkClick.aspx?fileticket=eCNg9MQW0UU%3D&tabid=315Hare, P.H. (1991).

The Echo Housing/Granny Flat Experience in the US. *Journal of Housing for the Elderly,* 7:2, 57-70.

Law, S. (2010, July 15). Granny flats fuel building surge. *Portland Tribune.* Retrieved from www.portlandtribune.com

Lazarowich, N.M. (1991). Granny Flats in Canada. *Journal of Housing for the Elderly,* 7:2, 31-39.

Owen, Bruce. (2010, June 30). Province offers $35K to build 'granny flats'. *Winnipeg Free Press.* Retrieved from http://www.winnipegfreepress.com/local/province-offers-35k-to-build-granny-flats-97460284.html

Rhor, M. (2011, August 8). Builders cite rise in 'Mother-in-Law Suites'. *Associated Press.* Retrieved from www.aarp.org.

Sperber, R. (1993). Taking granny (flats) to market. *Professional Builder,* 70:1, 179.

Stromberg, M. (2005). Designing Granny Flats. *Professional Builder,* 70:1, 171.

Sutro, D. (1997, May 18). Suite Success; The venerable 'granny flat' is being reborn as buyers and home builders explore ways to house today's evolving families. *Los Angeles Times,* K1-K2.

Tinker, A. (1991). Granny Flats – The British Experience. *Journal of Housing for the Elderly,* 7:2, 41-56.

Vancouver Sun. (1987, Oct 14). New 'granny flats' offer benefits to whole families. H10. Retrieved from http://search.proquest.com/docview/243720198?accountid=14771

Wiener, E. (1992, October 22). Granny Flat Zoning Proposal Draws Fire. *The Washington Post,* J01.

Agrell, S. (July 15, 2011). Rethinking Public Space – One Day at a Time. The Globe and Mail, A8-A9.

Agrell, S. and Yukselir, M. (August 22, 2011). Off-road living: curbing our cars. The Globe and Mail, A6-A7.

Applied Research Associates Inc. (2007). Estimation of Road Cost Allocation Between Light Vehicles and Heavy Vehicles in Canada. *Toronto: Applied Reaserch Associates Inc.*

Applied Research Associates Inc. (2008). Estimation of the Representative Annualized Capital and Maintenance Costs of Roads by Functional Class. *Toronto: Applied Research Associates Inc.*

Arduin, J.P. (1994). Development and Economic Evaluation of High Speed in France. *Japan Railway & Transport Review,* 26-31.

Auditor General Victoria. (2005). Franchising Melbourne's train and tram system. *Melbourne: Victorian Government Printer,* 15-34.

Bageen, S. (2007) Brand Dubai: The Instant City or Instantly Recognizable City. *International Planning Studie,.* 12(2), 173-197.

Bedford, P. (2005) Steering the Good Ship Intensification. *The Ontario Planning Journal,* 20(4): 17-18.

Bedford, P. (2008) Go Bold or Go Home. *The Ontario Planning Journal,* (23)3, 28-29.

Bedford P. (200x) All about Mixed Use. *The Ontario Planning Journal,* (24)4: 20-22

Bedoyere, C., & Powers, A. (2005). *Art Deco.* Old Saybrook, CT: Konecky & Konecky

Bennett, S. (1998). Crime, Order and Policing: Paradigmatic Disaster: The Crash of TWA Flight 800. *Scarman Centre for the Study of Public Order: University of Leicester, Occasional Paper No.13.*

Berman, D. (1999). Put a lid on it. *Canadian Business.* 71 (21): 19-20.

Bernstein, M. (1998). Sports Stadium Boondoggle. *Public Interest.* 132:45.

Black, J., and Lloyd, M. (1994). Football Stadia Developments: Land-use policy and planning controls. *The Town Planning Review.* 65 (1):1-19.

Borden, J. (1996). Crack in McDome Logic. *Crain's Chicago Business.* 19(10): 1.

Borrows, J. (1997) Living Between Water and Rocks: First Nations, environmental planning and democracy. *University of Toronto Law Journal,* 47(4), 417-468.

Bou, E. (1999). Churches and streetcars in Barcelona: Ways to modernity. *Romance Quarterly,* 204-215.

Brenner, N., & Theodore, N. (2002) Cities and Geographies of Actually Existing Neo-liberalism *Antipode,* 349-379.

Briggs, X. (1998) Doing Democracy Up-close: Culture, power, and communication in community building, *Journal of Planning Education and Research*, 18(1), 1-13.

Brinckerhoff, P. (2008). Ridership and Revenue Forecasts: California High-Speed Train Project. California High Speed Rail Authority. *Ridership and Revenue*, 1-11.

Brym, R.J. (2001). *Society in Question: Sociological Readings for the 21st Century (Third Edition)*. Toronto, ON: Harcourt Canada.

Bunting, T., & Filion P.(edited). (2000). Canadian Cities in Transition: the twenty-first century (2nd Edition). Don Mills, ON: Oxford University Press.

California High-Speed Rail Authority. (2008). *California High-Speed Train Business Plan*. Sacramento, CA.

Cambridge Systematics. (2008). Benefit Cost Analysis. *Sacramento: California High-Speed Rail Authority*.

Cambridge Systematics. (2008). Technical Documentation of the Benefit-Cost Analysis for the 2008 Business Plan. *Sacramento: California High-Speed Rail Authority*.

Campbell, S. (1996). Green Cities, Growing Cities, Just Cities. Urban Planning and the Contradictions of Sustainable Development. *Journal of the American Planning Association*, 26(3), 296-312.

Campos, J., & Rus, G.D. (2009). Some stylized facts about high-speed rail: A review of HSR experiences around the world. *Transport Policy*, 19-28.

Caro, R.A. (1975). *The Power Broker: Robert Moses and the Fall of New York*. New York, NY: Vintage Books: A Division of Random House.

Chien, S and Korikanthimath, V. (2007). Analysis and Modeling of Simultaneous and Staged Emergency Evacuations. *Journal of Transportation and Engineering*.

Christman, H.M. (edited). (1963). *Walt Whitman's New York: From Manhattan to Montauk*. Lanham, MD: New Amsterdam Books.

Chrystal, J. (2004). The Taj Mahal of Sport: The Creation of the Houston Astrodome. (Doctoral Dissertation). Iowa State University: Ames, Iowa.

City of Mississauga. Mississauga Train Derailment (1979). Retrieved from http://www.mississauga.ca/portal/residents/localhistory?paf_gear_id=9700018&itemId=5500001

City of Toronto. (2009.) City of Toronto Emergency Plan.

Clark, W. (2000). Traffic report: Weekday commuting patterns. *Canadian Social Trends*, 18-22.

Collard, E.A. (1962). *Montreal Yesterdays*. Toronto, ON: Longmans Canada Ltd.

Coto-Millan, P., Inglada, V., Rey, B. (2007). Effects of network economies in high-speed rail: the Spanish case. *Annals of Regional Science*, 911-925.

County of Simcoe. (2008) Final Report: County of Simcoe Transportation Master Plan. 181 pages.

County of Simcoe. (2008). Proposed Official Plan of the County of Simcoe.

Creswell, J. (2003). *Research Design (2nd Edition)*. Thousand Oaks. London. New Delhi: Sage Publications.

Croome, P., & Wallace, K. (2009, November 17). Metrolinx touts private sector for Transit City. *The National Post*.

Darling-Hammond, Linda, et al. *Reinventing High School: Outcomes of the Coalition Campus Schools Project*. American Education Research Journal, Fall 2002, Vol.39, No.3, pp. 639-673.

Davidoff, P. (1965) Advocacy and pluralism in planning. *A. Faludi (ed.) A Reader in Planning Theory*, 277-296.

Dear, M. (2000) The Postmodern Urban Condition *Deconstructing Urban Planning Ch. 6* Massachusetts: Blackwell, 117-139.

Donnelly, Steve. *The Next Steps in Community Collaborations*. School Planning and Management, Aug 2004.

Doré, G., Drouin, P., Pierre, P., & Desrochers, P. (2005). Estimation of the Relationships of Road Deterioration to Traffic and Weather in Canada. *Transport Canada*.

Dranitsaris, S. (2011). Email to Allan Bonner on August 9, 2011.

Economic Analysis Directorate. (2005). Interim Estimate of the Financial Costs and Revenues Associated with the Provision of Road Infrastructure in Canada, Provincial Estimates, 2000. *Transport Canada*.

Economic Analysis Policy Group. (2003). Investigation of the Full Costs of Transporation: A Discussion Paper. *Transport Canada*.

"Edison School/Pacific Park Project." *Case Studies: Joint Use*. New Schools Better Neighborhoods website. Available at: http://www.nsbn.org/case/jointuse/edison.php. [Accessed September 2010].

Egan, T. (July 24, 2011). What we can learn from Carmageddon. *The New York Times*, p. 10.

English, J. (2009). *The Downtown Relief Line Proposal. Transit Toronto February 2009*. Retrieved from http://transit.toronto.on.ca/subway/5113.shtml

Environment Canada. (2011). "Canada's top ten weather stories of 1998." http://www.ec.gc.ca/meteo-weather/default.asp?lang=En&n=3DED7A35-1#t1

Erenhalt, A. (2008). Trading Places: The demographic inversion of the American City. *The New Republic*.

Etzioni, A. (1967). Mixed-scanning: A 'Third' Approach to Decision-making. *Public Administration Review* 27(5), 385-392.

Fishman, R. (1977). Urban utopias: Ebenezer Howard and Le Corbusier. *S. Campbell and S. Fainstein (eds.) Readings in Planning Theory. Oxford: Blackwell*, 19-31.

Fausto Marincioni, F.A. (2009). The Lyon-Turin High-Speed Rail: The Public Debate and Perception of Environmental Risk in Susa Valley, Italy. *Environmental Management*, 863-875.

"Feasibility Study." American School & University, Vol.77, Iss.11, p.14, June 2005.

Federal Railroad Administration. (2009). Vision for High-Speed Rail in America. *Washington DC: US Department of Transportation.*

Ferg, B.F. (2007). *New York City Politics: Governing Gotham.* New Brunswick, New Jersey, and London: Rutgers University Press.

Flint, A. (2009). *Wrestling with Moses: How Jane Jacobs Took On New York's Master Builder and Transformed the American City.* New York, NY: Random House.

Florida, R. (2005). *Cities and the Creative Class.* New York. London: Routledge.

Forester, J. (1989). Planning in the face of power. *Planning in the Face of Power. Berkeley: University of California Press*, 27-47.

French, H. (1998). *Architecture: A Crash Course.* Vancouver, BC: Raincoast Books.

Freeman, S. and Taylor, B. (Aug 11, 2008). Residents return after blast. *The Toronto Star.* Retrieved from http://www.thestar.com/News/GTA/article/475696

Friedman, J. (1987). *Planning in the Public Domain: From Knowledge to Action.* Princeton, NJ: Princeton University Press.

Gabor, A. & Lewinberg, F. (1997). Zoning: New Urbanism. *Plan Canada, Vol. 38, No.4*, 12-17.

Grant, J. (2002). Mixed Use in Theory and Practice. Canadian Experience with implementing a Planning Principle. *Journal of American Planning Association*, 68(1), 71-84.

Grant, J. (editor) (2008). A Reader in Canadian Planning *Ch 14 The Tools of the Trade & Ch 15 Debates about Growth Dalhousie University: Thompson.* 339-358; 367-390.

Hall, P. (1988). *Cities of Tomorrow (3rd Edition).* Malden, MA: Blackwell Publishing.

Hamill, P. (2004). *Downtown: My Manhattan.* New York. Boston: Back Bay Books. Little Brown & Company.

Han, L, Yuan, F, and Chin, S-M. (2006) Global Optimization of Emergency Evacuation Assignments. *Interfaces*, 36(6): 502-513.

Han, L., Yuan, F, and Urbanik II, T. (2007). What is an effective evacuation operation? *Journal of Urban Planning and Development.*

Hanes, A. (2009, November 17). TTC to talk Eglinton line, critics wary. *The National Post.* A13.

Harcourt, M., & Cameron, K. with Rossiter, S. (2007). *City Making in Paradise: Nine Decisions that Saved Vancouver.* Vancouver and Toronto: Douglas & McIntyre.

Harris, G. (March 21, 2011). Dangers of Leaving No Resident Behind. *The New York Times.*

Harvard Business School Press (2000). *Harvard Business Review on Business and the Environment.* Boston, MA: A Harvard Business Review Paperback.

Harvard Business School Press (1999). *Harvard Business Review on Corporate Strategy.* Boston, MA: A Harvard Business Review Paperback.

Harvard Business School Press (2000). *Harvard Business Review on Negotiation and Conflict Resolution.* Boston, MA: A Harvard Business Review Paperback.

Harvard Business School Press (1998). *Harvard Business Review on Strategies for Growth.* Boston, MA: A Harvard Business Review Paperback.

Harvey, D. (1989). From managerialism to entrepreneurialism: the transformation of urban governance. *Geografiska Annaler*, 71(1), 3-17.

Harvey, D. (n.d.) Materializations of Utopias of Spatial Form. *Possible Urban Worlds*, 65-71.

Harvey, D. (1997). New Urbanism and the Communitarian Trap. *Harvard Design Magazine*, 1-3.

Harvey, D. (1978). On Planning the Ideology of Planning. *R. Burchell and G. Sternlieb (eds.) Planning Theory in the 1980s. Center for Urban Policy Research: New, Brunswick, New Jersey.*

Harvey, D. (2003). The Right to the City. *International Journal of Urban and Regional Research* 27(4), 939-941.

Hatton, Elizabeth J. *Charles Sturt University: A Case Study of Institutional Amalgamation.* Higher Education 44, pp 5-27, 2002.

Healy, P. (1992). Planning Through Debate: the communicative turn in planning theory. *Town Planning Review*, 63(2), 367-384.

Healey, P. (1997). Traditions of planning thought. *Chapter 1 in Collaborative Planning: Shaping Places in Fragmented Societies. Vancouver: UBC Press*, 7-30.

Hedelin, A., Bunketorp, O., and Björnstig, U. (2002). Public transport in metropolitan areas – a danger for unprotected road users. *Safety Science, Volume 40, Issue 5, July 2002*, 467-477.

Heisz, A., & LaRochelle-Côté, S. (2005). Getting to work. *Canadian Social Trends*, 14-17.

Holston, J. (1989) Chapter 1: Premises and Paradoxes, Chapter 2: Blueprint Utopia, & Chapter 3: The Plans Hidden Agenda. *The Modernist City Chicago.* London: University of Chicago.

Hopkins, T.H. (2001). A Nationwide High-Speed Monorail Grid for the United States. *The Monorail Society.*

HurricaneHazel.ca (2004) Index. Retrieved from www.hurricanehazel.ca

Huxley, M. (2000). The limits to communicative planning. *Journal of Planning Education and Research,* 19(4), 369–377.

Infrastructure Management Group Inc. (2008). Financial Plan for the California High Speed Rail Authority San Francisco to Anaheim Segment. *Sacramento: California High Speed Rail Authority.*

Infrastructure Management Group Inc. (2008). Report of Responses to the Request for Expression of Interest for Private Participation in the development of a High Speed Train System in California. Sacramento, CA: *Californai High Speed Rail Authority.*

Isin, E., & Siemiatycki, M. (1999) Fate and Faith. Claiming Urban Citizenship in Immigrant Toronto. *Working Paper Series #8 CERIS 30p.*

Jacobs, J. (1992). *The Death and Life of Great American Cities.* New York, NY: Vintage Books, A Division of Random House, Inc.

Jakes, A.S. (n.d.). Economic Analysis of a Monorail between The Stratosphere Tower and Downtown Las Vegas. *The Monorail Society* .

*Jeremiah E. Burke High School.* Schwartz/Silver Architects. Architectural Record: Vol. 198 Issue 1, p38, Jan 2010.

Kennedy, R.R. (n.d.). Considering Monorail Rapid Transit for North American Cities. *The Monorail Society.*

Kennedy, M. (1996). Transformative Community Planning: Empowerment through Community Development. *Planners Network,* 117.

Kiefer, J., and Montjoy, R. (2006). Incrementalism before the Storm: Network Performance for the Evacuation of New Orleans. *Public Administration review.* Special Issue: 122-130.

Knox, P.L., & Taylor, P.J. (edited). (1995). *World Cities in a World-System.* New York, NY: Cambridge University Press.

Krumholz, N. (1982). A retrospective view of equity planning: Cleveland, 1969-1979. *Journal of the American Planning Association,* 48(2), 163-183.

Kuitenbrouwer, P. (2009, January 10). How Toronto went cold on subways. *The National Post.* A11.

Krumholz, N. (1990). To be Professionally Effective, be Politically Articulate. *Krumholz and Forester (eds.) Making Equity Planning Work.*

Kunstler, J.H. (1993). *The Geography of Nowhere: the Rise and Decline of America's Man-Made Landscape.* New York, NY: A Touchstone Book Published by Simon & Schuster.

Kuwabara, T., Hiraishi, M., Goda, K., Okamoto, S., Ito, A., & Sugita, Y. (n.d.). New Solution for Urban Traffic: Small-type Monorail System. *The Monorail Society* . Tokyo, Japan: The Monorail Society.

Lam, V., & Lee, C. (2006). *The Flu Pandemic and You: A Canadian Guide.* Canada: Doubleday Canada.

Larner, W., and D. Craig (2005). After Neo-liberalism? Community Activism and Local Partnerships in Aotearoa New Zealand. *Antipode,* 402-424.

Lash, S., Szerszynki, B. & Wynne. B (edited). (1996). *Risk, Environment & Modernity: Towards a New Ecology.* London. Thousand Oaks. New Delhi: Sage Publications.

Leslie, D. (2005). Creative Cities? *Geoforum,* 36, 403-405.

Lindblom, C. (1959). The Science of 'Muddling Through'. *Public Administration Review* 19: 79-88 (Campbell and Fainstein, 288-304).

Little Bear, L. (2004). Aboriginal Paradigms: Implications for relationships to land and treaty making. *Wilkins, K. ed. Advancing Aboriginal Claims: Visions / Strategies / Directions. Purich,* 26-38.

Loeb, A. (2005). *The Condominium Act: A User's Manual (2ⁿᵈ Edition).* Toronto, ON: Thomson Canada Ltd.

López Pita, A., Bachiller, A., Teixeira, P.F., Casas-Espulgas, C., Insa, R. (2008). Iberian rail: adding a new dimension to international travel. *Transport,* 2008, Vol 161; Issue 2, 77-83.

Lorimer, J. (1972). *A Citizen's Guide to City Politics.* Toronto, ON: James Lewis & Samuel.

Lorimer, J. (1978). *The Developers.* Toronto, ON: James Lorimer & Company, Publishers.

Matthews, Kaye. *The Critical Success Factors for School and Community Joint Use Libraries in New Zealand.* Aplis 21(1), March 2008.

McHugh, K, and Meister, R. (2004). Campus-Public Partnerships: Successful Models for Strategic and Facilities Planning. *Change,* 36(5):22-30.

McLean, Russ. *Seven Red Herrings: The Opposition to Closure of Aging Urban Schools.* The Clearing House, Vol.76, No.3, pp140-142, January/February 2003.

Ministry of Industry. (2006). Guide to Transportation Data. *Ottawa: Statistics Canada.*

Metro Transport Sydney Pty Ltd. Technical Documents for Monorail. *Sydney: Metro Transport Sydney Pty Ltd.*

Melek, M., Shlemon, E., Zekioglu, A., and Carter, S. (2007). The Portland Aerial Transportation, Inc. *STRUCTURE Magazine,* 34-36.

Millward, R. and Associates. (2010). Co-location precedents in North America.

Ministry of Industry. (2008). Commuting Patterns and Places of Work of Canadians, 2006 Census. *Ottawa: Statistics Canada*.

Ministry of Industry. (2006). Guide to Transportation Data. *Ottawa: Statistics Canada*.

Ministry of Transportation (2007). Transportation Trends and Outlooks for the Greater Toronto Area and Hamilton: Need and Opportunities Draft Report. *IBI Group, 76*.

MMM Group. (2006). Greater Toronto Area Cordon Count Program Transportation Trends 1991-2006. *Toronto: Joint Program in Transportation University of Toronto Data Management Group*.

Moshe G., & Banister, D. (2007). Role of the Railways in the Future of Air Transport. *Transportation Planning & Technology*, 95-112.

Ontario (2005). *Greenbelt Plan 2005*. Ministry of Municipal Affairs and Housing.

Mutch, R, et al. (2010). Protecting Lives and Property in the Wildland-Urban Interface: Communities in Montana and Southern California adopt Australian Paradigm. *Fire Technology*, 47: 357-377.

Ontario (2002). *Oak Ridges Moraine Conservation Plan*. Toronto, ON: Ministry of Municipal Affairs and Housing.

Ontario (2006). Ontario Heritage Tool Kit: Heritage Property Evaluation, Municipal Heritage Committees, Heritage Conservation Districts, Designating Heritage Properties.

Ontario. (2007). Southern Highways Program 2007 to 2011. Toronto, ON.

Osbaldeston, M. (2008). *Unbuilt Toronto: A History of the City That Might Have Been*. Toronto, ON: Dundurn Press.

O'Toole, Megan. (March 30, 2010) Toronto overtakes LA in gridlock. *The National Post*.

PBS DVD Gold (1999). *New York: A Documentary Film. Episode 1-7*.

Pfeiffer, B.B. & Nordland, G. (1988). *Frank Lloyd Wright in the Realm of Ideas*. Carbondale and Edwardsville: Southern Illinois University Press.

Portland Aerial Tram. (2007). 2007 Annual Report. *Portland, Oregon: City of Portland*.

Portland Aerial Transportation Inc. (2004). Portland Aerial Tram: Final Recommendation and Report. *Portland, Oregon*.

Prévost, R. (1991). *Montreal: A History (translated by Elizabeth Mueller and Robert Chodos)*. Montreal, QC: McClelland & Stewart Inc.

Pulido, L. (2000). Rethinking Environmental Racism: White Privilege and Urban Development in Southern California. *Annals of the Association of American Geographers*, 90(1), 12-40.

Rasmussen, S.E. (1959). *Experiencing Architecture*. Cambridge, MA: The MIT Press: Massachusetts Institute of Technology.

Reardon, K.M. (2008) Participatory Neighborhood Planning for Community Renewal: A Bottom-Up, Bottom-Sideways Approach to Practice. *The Introduction to Community Development, edited by Rhonda A. Philips and Robert Pittman, London: Routledge/Taylor and Francis Group*.

Reiss, S. (1998). Historical Perspectives on Sport and Public Policy. *Policy Studies Review*. 15(1): 3-15.

Riis, J. (1997). *How the Other Half Lives*. New York, NY: Penguin Books.

Ripley, A. (Feb 28, 2009) Run for your lives, please. Retrieved from http://governing .com

Romeo, Jim. *The ABCs of Mixed Use Schools*. Planning, Vol. 70, Iss. 7, p.4-10, Jul 2004.

Rose, Alex, et al. "The Development of Educational Facilities through Joint Use Mechanisms." *Case Studies: Joint Use*. New Schools Better Neighborhoods website. Available at: http://www.nsbn.org/case/jointuse /developfacilities.php. [Accessed September 2010].

Roy, F. (2008). From Roads to Rinks: Government Spending on Infrastructure in Canada, 1961 to 2005. *Canadian Economic Observer, Statistics Canada. September 2007*.

Rumsey, D. (2003). *Statistics for Dummies*. Hoboken, NJ: Wiley Publishing Inc.

Rusk, J. (2006, May 5). Caledonia land dispute is spilling over. *The Globe and Mail*, A18.

Rust-D'Eye, G. & Bar-Moshe, O. (2009). *The Ontario Municipal Act: A User's Manual -2009*. Thomson Carswell.

Sacramento Area Council of Governments. (2006). Road Maintenance. *Sacramento*.

Sager, Don. *Changing Perspectives: Joint Use of Facilities by Schools and Public Libraries*. Public Libraries 38, No. 6 (355-359), Nov-Dec 1999.

Sandercock, L. (2003). *Cosmopolis II: Mongrel Cities in the 21st Century*. London. New York: Continuum.

Sandercock, L. (1998). *Towards Cosmopolis*. Chichester. New York. Weinheim. Brisbane. Singapore. Toronto: John Wiley & Sons.

Sassen, S. (1991). *The Global City: New York, London, Tokyo*. Princeton, NJ: Princeton University Press.

Schindler, H. (1981). Concerning the Origin of the Onion Dome and Onion Spires in Central European Architecture. *Journal of the Society of Architectural Historians*. 40(2):138-142.

Scott, J.C. (1998). *Seeing Like a State: How Certain Schemes to Improve the Human Condition Have Failed*. New Haven and London: Yale University Press.

Soberman, R. (2008). *Preliminary Analysis of Fast Ferry Services to Downtown Toronto from Scarborough and Etobicoke*. Conducted for the Toronto Transit Commission. 22 pages.

Starbird, M. (2006). *Meaning from Data: Statistics Made Clear Part II*. Chantilly, VA: The Teaching Company.

Statistics Canada. (2007). Canadian Economic Observer. *Ottawa: Ministry of Industry*.

Statistics Canada. (2006). The Canadian Passenger Bus and Urban Transit Industries.

Statistics Canada. (2006). Rail in Canada. *Ottawa: Ministry of Industry*.

Statistics Canada. (2001). 2001 Census Place of Work, Greater Toronto Area and Hamilton Summary. *Ottawa: Statistics Canada*.

Statistics Canada. (2009). *2006 Community Profile*. Retrieved from http://www12.statcan.ca/census-recensement/2006/dp-pd/prof/92591/details/page.cfm?Lang=E&Geo1=CSD&Code1=3518013&Geo2=PR&Code2=35&Data=Count&SearchText=Oshawa&SearchType=Begins&SearchPR=35&B1=All&Custom=

Statistics Canada. (2009). *2006 Community Profile*. Retrieved from http://www12.statcan.ca/census-recensement/2006/dp-pd/prof/92-591/details/Page.cfm?Lang=E&Geo1=CSD&Code1=3524001&Geo2=PR&Code2=35&Data=Count&SearchText=Oakville&SearchType=Begins&SearchPR=35&B1=All&Custom=

Statistics Canada. (2008). *The Canadian Passenger Bus and Urban Transit Industries*. Retrieved from http://www.statcan.gc.ca/cgi-bin/af-fdr.cgi?l=eng&loc=http://www.statcan.gc.ca/pub/50-002-x/50-002-x2008001-eng.pdf&t=The%20Canadian%20Passenger%20Bus%20and%20Urban%20Transit%20Industries%20(Service%20Bulletin%20-%20Surface%20and%20Marine%20Transport)

Straw, J. (2011) Mass Evacuation: A Disaster waiting to Happen. *Security management:* http://www.security-management.com

Strupat, B. The Suburbs need to smarten up. *The Globe and Mail.*

Surface and Marine Transport. (2006). The Canadian passenger bus and urban transit industries, 2004 (Preliminary) and 2003 (Final). *Ottawa: Statistics Canada.*

Sydney Ferries. (2008). Sydney Ferries Annual Report 2007-2008. *Sydney, NSW, Australia.*

Talen, E. (2008) New Urbanism, Social Equity and the Challenge of Post-Katrina Rebuilding in Mississippi. *Journal of Planning Education and Research, 27,* 277-293.

The Greater Astoria Historical Society and the Roosevelt Island Historical Society (2008). *Images of America: The Queensboro Bridge.* Charleston SC, Chicago IL, Portsmouth NH, San Francisco CA: Arcadia Publishing.

The Roosevelt Island Operating Corporation. (2009). Financial Statements and Management's Discussion and Analysis. *New York.*

The New York Times Magazine (2009, June 14). The Architecture Issue: Infrastructure!.

Toronto Transit Commission. (2009, November) *Commuter Ferry Service*. 3 pages.

Toronto Transit Commision. (2007). Annual Report. *Toronto: Toronto Transit Commission.*

Toronto Transit Commission. (2003, March) *Ridership Growth Strategy.* P. 9.

TorontoGasPrices.com. (2009). *Prices Nationally*. Retrieved May 14, 2009, from Toronto Gas Prices: http://www.torontogasprices.com/Prices_nationally.aspx

Township of Springwater Official Plan.

Traffic Office. (1988-2005). Provincial Highways Traffic Volumes 1988-2005. *Ottawa: Ministry of Transportation.*

Traffic Office. (2005). Provincial Highways Traffic Volumes 2005 (AADT Only). *Ottawa: Ministry of Transportation.*

Transportation Services. (2006, December 31). *City of Toronto: Transportation Services.* Retrieved May 14, 2009, from City of Toronto Web site: http://www.toronto.ca/transportation/publications/brochures/2006volmap.pdf

Ullman, E. (1954) Amenities as a Factor in Regional Growth. *Geographical Review.* 44(1): 119-132.

Vincent, Jeffrey M. *Planning and Siting New Public Schools in the Context of Cimmunity Development: The California Experience.* (Doctoral Dissertation, University of California, Berkeley, 2006).

Virginia Department of Transportation. (2006, Oct 29). *Ferry Boat Feasibility Study.* Retrieved May 20, 2009, from Virginia Department of Transportation Projects and Studies: http://www.virginiadot.org/projects/studynova-ferry.asp

Walsh, K. (2006). *Forgotten New York: View of a Lost Metropolis.* New York, NY: HarperCollins Publishers.

Weber R. (2002) Extracting value from Cities. Neo-libralism and Urban Redevelopment. *Antipode,* 519-540.

Wells, G. (2006). Tracking a Mass Evacuation.

Wickens, S. (2011). "TTC makes 'dumbest decision ever,' former head warns." The Globe and Mail.

Wilson-Smith, A. et al. (1998). Great Ice Storm of 1998. Retrieved from http://www.thecanadianencyclopedia.com/index.cfm?PgNm=TCE&Params=M1ARTM0011472

Wirth, L. (1964). *On Cities and Social Life: Selected Papers, Edited and an Introduction by Albert J. Reiss Jr.* The Heritage of Sociology. Chicago and London: Phoenix Books, The University of Chicago Press.

Wheeler, M. (2000). *Teaching Negotiations: Ideas and Innovations.* Cambridge, MA: PON Books.

Wood, D.H. (2008). *The Planning ACT: A Source Books (6th Edition).* Toronto, ON: Thomson Canada Ltd.

Yiftachel, O. (1994). The Dark Side of Modernism: Planning as control of an ethnic minority. *Watson, S. and Gibson, K. (eds.) Postmodern Cities and Spaces.* London, Blackwell, 216-241.

Zhang, L. (2006). Contesting Spatial Modernity in Late-Socialist China. *Current Anthropology,* 47(3), 461-484.

Zimbalist, A. (1998). The Economics of Stadiums, Teams and Cities. *Policy Studies Review.* 15(1):17-29.

# INTERVIEWEES & READERS

Dr. Ron Woznow, CEO AFMNet, (Advanced Food and Materials Network–Federal Centre of Excellence, Guelph). Initiator, Healthy City initiative.

David McFadden, partner, Gowlings, founding chair, Environics Research, Chair Ontario Centres of Excellence, Toronto Board of Trade, infrastructure specialist, Chair, consortium (Alstom, Aecon, Borealis Infrastructure) 3P project to bring LRT system to Toronto on existing rail lines and hydro corridors.

Robert Millward, Consultant, former Commissioner of Planning and Development, City of Toronto.

Senator Art Eggleton, Chair, Senate Sub-Committee on cities. Former Mayor of Toronto.

Chris Hume, Art, Architecture & Planning columnist, Toronto Star.

Rollo Myers, Manager, Architectural Conservancy of Ontario, Jane Jacobs Prize Winner.

# Photo Credits

This book is a non-commercial, educational project. It has received some assistance through the not-for-profit urban development organization, Artscape, which deemed me and a small team of researchers qualified to use a cost-effective office for our work.

We have taken all possible care in the selection and use of images in this book. We have made best efforts to contact photographers and organizations responsible for the images for permission to user their work. If you see an error we've made, let us know.

We reproduce some of these images in the spirit of fair use for educational purposes and as excerpts from larger photographic competitions, exhibits and shows to promote the artists and institutions involved. Thanks to the Institute for Transportation and Development Policy and their *Our Cities Ourselves: Vision 2030* exhibition for providing the cover image for this book, and for providing many concept drawings of a bright urban future.

Recent exhibits at MOMA, The Cooper-Hewitt, The Museum of the City of New York, The Skyscraper Museum and New York's Center for Architecture have helped inspire this work. We also acknowledge the three recent retrospectives on Robert Moses at Columbia University, Flushing Meadows and The Museum of the City of New York.

We are grateful for all those who provided support and inspiration.

# Special Photo Credits

Making this book come to life has been made possible by the generosity of people and organizations across the globe whose visions of a safer, more resilient, and sustainable world have been reproduced here. We would ask that if you have further interest in the work of the organizations listed, to engage with them though the contact information below.

**Vincent Callebaut Architectures**
2, rue de la Roquette
Passage du Cheval Blanc, Cour de Mars
75011 Paris
France
Phone: 0033 1 43 43 08 56
Email: vincent@callebaut.org
Website: www.vincent.callebaut.org

**Institute for Transportation and Development Policy Headquarters**
9 East 19th Street, 7th Floor
New York, NY 10003
Phone: 1 212 629 8001
Email: mobility@itdp.org
Website: https://www.itdp.org/

**Waterfront Toronto**
20 Bay Street, Suite 1310
Toronto, ON M5J 2N8
Phone: 1 416 214 1344
Email: info@waterfrontoronto.ca
Website: http://www.waterfrontoronto.ca/

**Q Drum**
PO Box 53059, Troyeville, 2139
Johannesburg, South Africa
Phone: 27 0 11 624 6700
Email: info@qdrum.co.za
Website: www.qdrum.co.za

**GeoStrut North America**
1374 West 200 South
Lindon, UT 84042
contact@geostrut.com
Phone: 801 356 1311

**QPGS Architects**
Quentin Perchet and Gabriel Scerri
Email: contact@qpgsarchitects.com
Website: http://cargocollective.com/qpgsarchitects

**The Gondola Project**
Email: gondola@creativeurbanprojects.com
Website: http://gondolaproject.com/